GOD PICKS UP THE PIECES

GOD PICKS UP THE PIECES

Ecclesiastes:
The words of Qohelet,
a son of David,
who was a King in Jerusalem

CALVIN G. SEERVELD

DORDT PRESS

Dordt Press   www.dordt.edu/dordt-press-catalog
700 7th St NE
Sioux Center, Iowa 51250

ISBN: 978-0-932914-16-3

Printed in the United States of America.

The Library of Congress Cataloguing-in-Publication Data is on file with the Library of Congress, Washington D.C.

Library of Congress Control Number: 2023932937

Scripture translations, unless noted otherwise, are the author's responsibility.

Cover image: Antonio Soto, *Vanidades* (or *El Don*), 2006
painting, 130x 96cm, collection of the artist, Spain.

Comment by the artist (translated by Joyce Philips): The struggle, or life, which is the same, casts its doubts, its shadows. The whirlwind surrounds you, envelops you. You are the center and feel powerful. But you find impossible voids to fill; hollow, incomplete forms; spaces of nothingness; vanity, vanity of vanities.

Comment by the author of this book:

> We humans can be buckled-over, broken people.
> But we live in God's world of sunlight, blue and green,
> touched by red.
> When old and tired, we drop things.
> Yet God picks up the pieces of our lives.

Dedicated to my wife, Inès
(1931-2021 AD),
a woman of sturdy tenderness
to whom I owe my working life,
who stood beside me all these Qohelet years
as a Woman Wisdom.

TABLE OF CONTENTS

1
PREFACE

Just as the biblical book of *Job* is largely a back-and-forth dialogical dispute between Job and his three friends, the biblical book of *Ecclesiastes* is largely a back-and-forth rhetorical questioning and provisional answering monologue by a Qohelet figure. And just as in the book of *Job* other voices enter the dialogue—as Job's wife, later a strange Elihu, and finally God's direct voice, so there are other voices in the book of *Ecclesiastes* too—an editor, a Woman Wisdom voice, and a couple of Proverb-quoting, apprentice rabbi figures trying out their contributions to godly "wisdom."

At least this is one good way to take seriously the literary form of the canonic text and recognize that *Ecclesiastes* is a piece of biblical "wisdom literature." *Ecclesiastes* is not a straightforward dogmatic treatise like *Leviticus* or an historical narrative like the Bible books named "Samuel." *Ecclesiastes* is not like Luke's report called "The Acts of the Apostles" or written like a letter the apostle Paul sent to the church congregations at Corinth. *Ecclesiastes* is more like an imaginative collection of poetic Psalms and perceptive Proverbs spelling out, with give-and-take flair, how to live well on earth before God, or foolishly.

When Robert Estienne's versification of the Bible in the 1550s AD became a popular standard procedure, it became easier for anybody to refer to a given passage somewhere in the Bible. But versification also came to atomize the reading of holy Scripture. People think the Bible is made up of verses instead of being a *true-story narrative*. But if you lose the paragraph context of a verse or neglect the whole book wrappings of a chapter or paragraph of a verse, you are setting yourself up to misread the meaning of a Bible text out of its context. Then a person is tempted to proof-text Scripture the way the devil did when he tempted Jesus Christ in the wilderness (Luke 4:1-13).

Further, when biblical doctrines became so important that heresy (for example, purgatorial clemency for money) led to the historical Reformation-separation from the Roman Catholic papal church, that action reinforced the practice, I think, to read the Bible in categorical fashion. The Bible became predominantly a dogmatics source book. You find in the Bible true dogma, which you need to believe in order to be saved, and you find anathematized in the Bible the doctrines that are false and need to be rejected. In my judgment, however, if a person reduces the Bible to its doctrinal backbone, one has lost the fleshed-out body of the gospel, its kerygmatic appeal to repent of your sin and to accept personally the communal adoption to be a child of the triune God, revealed in Jesus Christ.

Another general factor that has cramped Bible reading is the sea-change that happened around the 1700s AD, when reading a book became practised in silence. The Israelites at the time of Moses had God's word revealed to university-trained Moses, who wrote it down, and read it aloud to them at key festive times (Exodus 24:3-8, v.7; Deuteronomy 31:9-13; cf. also Joshua 8:32-35; II Kings 23:1-3; and Nehemiah 8:1-12). The apostle Paul's letters to congregations also were spoken to them by the elders, who were literate (1 Colossians 4:16; I Thessalonians 5:27; cf. also Acts 13:15 and Luke 4:16-21). And while general literacy, especially after the Gutenberg invention of the printing press, is a sound societal development, something important to the Bible is lost if its oral character is not practised. Holy Scripture, I believe, is meant especially to be heard, to be read aloud, alone or in community. The tone of a human voice is integral to the translation of God's Word received in the Hebraic, Aramaic, and Greek languages.

So this present book is an invitation to hear the *Ecclesiasates* Scripture as a unified chorus of different voices. The Qohelet voice assumes briefly, at the beginning of *Ecclesiastes*, a Solomon-like persona the way Christ adopts the voice of a Samaritan in telling the parable about "Who is my neighbour?" (Luke 10:25-37). There is a sevenfold refrain in *Ecclesiastes*, attesting to its whole as a unified script, the way a refrain shows that Psalm 42 and 43 are really one psalm (42:5,11 and 43:5). And at the end of the *Ecclesiastes* book, after a closing apocalyptic poem (12:1-7), there is a coda of voices commenting upon and summing up the entire point of the Wisdom-searching enterprise—"Stand in awe of God and keep God's commandments" (*Eccesiastes* 12:8-14)—almost like the epilogue to the Newer Testament book of *Revelation*, which emphasizes the point of its 22 chapters: I, Jesus, son of David, am coming soon as final Judge—get ready. (22:8-21)!

A brief note about my literary translation

I claim that my rendering of the original Hebrew is not a "paraphrase," like the brilliant work of Eugene Peterson's *The Message*, but hews something closer to the original Hebrew text as "a translation."

Yet my translation wants the pungent grit of Luther's rough-hewn German-folk version, open to the poetic imprint of judicious slang. God's Word is tenaciously direct, but richly nuanced and concretely imageic, rather than abstract; so the English equivalent should be both blunt and full of down-to-earth wiggle, playful. Every denotative word has a range of multiple connotations which, in poetry, come to the fore. Therefore expect a literary translation to be imaginative rather than prosaic.

For example: הבל (*hebel*), which Martin Buber translates as "Dunst" (fumes, 1952), is exactly right, imageic, and precise, like automobile exhaust. And it does not take much imagination to convert such obnoxious, wasteful, and gaseous fumes of *hebel* into a current borderline improper word like "fart." So, rather than whitewash הבל into a philosophical denigration such as "absurd" (Fox, 1989) or "meaningless" (Garrett, 1993) or even "enigmatic" (Bartholomew 2009), I use "fart" for the disgusting falsity Qohelet disappointedly announces to be the possible vain ("vanity") verdict for what all human effort amounts to.

Poetic variants I use for this stinking emptiness relevant to the specific occasion are "stinking worthless", "an overrated dream" (straining work that is always unsatisfying, 4:8), "a woeful, flagrantly empty, pernicious bitterness" (your hard-won affluence denied your enjoyment, 6:2), "claptrap" (pretentious insincere language, 6:11). הבל is an off-colour but not-quite-swearing interjective judgment for a fruitless, stymied wasteful production. It is close to Ezekiel's use of the term גלולימ for God-usurping idols, with commentary which prim Christians certainly find uncomfortable talk (Ezekiel 23:17-21). But such disgusting blunt terminology for proud human sinful deeds is, in my judgment, deeply biblical.

2

Oral introduction: Understanding the biblical book of *Ecclesiastes**

The Biblical book of *Ecclesiastes* highlights what it means to be a genuine, if troubled, believer. A document or an action is "genuine" when it is fully trustworthy as real, not adulterated. A matter is "genuine" when it is utterly true to its original nature in God's world, like actual maple syrup tapped from trees, a verified ancient manuscript, a promising kiss, or a bona fide declaration by an authority. The opposite of "genuine" is "counterfeit," "fake."

My task is to prepare you to hear the genuine Word of God booked in the Older Testament canonic writing called *Ecclesiastes*. I understand the Bible to be God-speaking literature, handed down historically to us today as a Holy-Spirited, Hebrew/Aramaic and Greek-scripted text, deemed authoritative for centuries by the Church for us/anybody to hear, on what's up or what's going on: How could/should we as human creatures live if we would be genuine before God on the face of the earth?

Rather than spend time reciting the many conflicting readings and misinterpretations of *Ecclesiastes*, let me tell you how and why we are going to read aloud/speak to you the entire 18-page, Hebrew-scripted piece, translated as a unified chorus of voices.

God-speaking literature

As I said, I believe the Bible is God-speaking literature. That should not surprise you if you know anything about the Bible story from the beginning in *Genesis* through the final section called the Apocalypse. The Bible is one continuous, interjected story telling about the LORD God's

---

*This is a 40-minute introduction, which was presented in the leisure of the Spanish Arts Gathering (2010) for questions and discussion a day before the book of *Ecclesiastes* was verbally performed for a listening audience. A shortened 15-minute version was used in other venues later, to give orientation for listeners who were then offered an aural presentation of the book.

great deeds and minute blessings in history: God upholds and quakes mountains, makes bees plant clover and the clouds water trees, oversees the birth of ostriches and whales (Psalm 104, Job 38-39), provides for and sometimes punishes fickle human creatures, who care for but often rape and murder one another generation after generation. This Bible story reveals God's ache to make people and the whole creation whole, filled with shalom—overflowing goodness—even if it costs God the death of God's son, Jesus Christ (John 3:16-21,v.17).

But my point now is: this true story told to those who can read has a defining literary quality. The Holy Spirit has more imagination than a bureaucrat. The Bible is not a government-issue bulletin: "Don't do this and don't do that; and if you be good, you'll go to heaven." That is not the genuine gospel. Instead, the biblical writings say that God in Jesus loves sinners! (Do you get that?) Followers of Jesus will live thankful if faulty lives until God comes through in the end. And this truth is proclaimed in storybook, literary-rich fashion.

God uses rainbows instead of a tersely dictated telegram to promise that no flooding catastrophe will be total anymore (Genesis 9:8-17). God instructed the prophet Nathan long ago to visit Israelite King David, who had orchestrated a murder to cover up his adultery with the wife, and tell David a made-up story about a rich man who bullied a poor neighbour and stole his one sheep; and when David said, "That fellow deserves to die," God's messenger, the wise Nathan, said, "You are that man, sir" (II Samuel 11-12).

Jesus told parables, which drove the conservatist Pharisees and the liberalist Sadducees to distraction and confused his own disciples (Matthew 13; 15:1-20; 22), because they all were accustomed to mind, as it were, the mono-syllables of communication, the bare literal letters rather than the literary-formulated message. That's been a problem for many theologicians too, who tend to reduce biblical-narrative and sparring-dialogue, psalmodic poetry to bare analytic dogmas, as if only logical, propositional prose can truly convey the disciplining and justifying mercy of God. Even Christians who unwittingly house a Positivist mentality and enjoy the factuality of Impressionist paintings can subvert the visions of Ezekiel or Daniel and the transcriptions of heaven seen by the apostle John on Patmos, and turn them into fixed time-tables, which God is apparently minding, although Jesus confidentially told a few of his closest, inquisitive disciples that even he did not know when the Final Reckoning of good and evil would take place (Mark 13:3-37).

A book of multiple voices

To put it simply, the book of *Ecclesiastes* is something like the book of *Job* in the Bible: that fantastic story of Satan's daring God to let the devil mess up God-fearing Job's life to see whether Job's trust in God was truly genuine or not. Then you have three bilious "friends" of Job trying to speechify him into admitting guilt for his suffering, i.e., that Job deserves the pain. Job remonstrates passionately and, pushed to the brink, says, "I know for certain that the One who shall ransom me, even after the worms get my corpse, lives! And I shall see God with my very own eyes. Would, though, that we busybody irascible humans could find a saving Wisdom..." (Job 19 and 28). And then a strange young Elihu pops up to set both Job's friends and Job himself straight, before the overpowering, just-doing, majestic Creator God (Job 32-37), until God self speaks up to end all the palaver by extolling God's marvelous wild animals (Job 40-41), whose ferocious doings should humble all Humanists' talk about Evil, with their genteel calculations, parsing out rewards and punishments. Job's friends—who get the most air time in the book— were dead wrong, says God; so Job had better pray for them to be saved (Job 42:7-9).

The biblical book of *Ecclesiastes* is as poetic, complicated, enigmatic, gripping, and deeply comforting—if you stay with it listening—as the book of *Job*, because you can come to hear God's compassionate, empathetic voice calling to you like the hidden ventriloquist through the different interacting circle of voices.

There is an **editor** (1:1,7:28, 8:1, 12:8), who refers to Qohelet, the intense, querulous man who, as resident philosopher, a wise man like Job, is trying to figure out what all the toil and trouble everywhere means. The editor frames the book with a prologue speech, which sums up the common problem: does not all our hard work end up evaporating, gone with the wind of human amnesia? All of you and your deeds will sooner or later be utterly forgotten, like dried-out grass blowin' in the wind (Isaiah 40:6-8).

Qohelet is the main speaker in the book, persistently probing the meaning of things. "Qohelet" means "leader of a qahal," an assembly of people gathered to learn from a teacher. Qohelet is like an imam in a mosque or a rabbi in a synagogue, a recognized "wise person," who fits into post-exile Israel's history after kings in the line of David were gone, after prophets like Malachi had faded into the misty past, while only a hereditary caste of Ezra-like priests counted out tithes and acted the role of kosher butchers for sacrificing in the temple. It is the time when the dispersed Jewish people were milling around aimlessly politically, and any leaders after Nehemiah could be wondering, "Have we forfeited our claim to be God's chosen people?"

There is also a **sevenfold refrain** in *Ecclesiastes,* which is the key to understanding the thrust of the ostensibly-questioning monologic cast of the piece. The refrain will be danced each time so that you recognize its recurrence and increasingly pivotal significance.

You will also meet a **WISDOM voice,** which utters some of the most searching, reflective, astute directional counsel in the book. The WISDOM voice sometimes coincides with the refrain and acts like the conscience of Qohelet, the bedrock, troubled, but certainly foundational affirmation of trust in God, for God does somehow pick up the broken pieces of our lives and history. The WISDOM voice is cast as that of a woman because Proverbs 1-9 speaks about authentic Woman Wisdom and the counterfeit of Woman Foolishness. Qohelet self in *Ecclesiastes* 7:28 laments—a follow-up to Job 28—that in all his detective searches he could not find and pin down Woman WISDOM.[1]

There are also a couple of **voices debating with proverbs** on which is "better" advice, if you want to know what is "good" for your daily life. You might think of it as young rabbis in training, jousting with one another—"Can you top this one?"—or playfully extending the other's metaphoric insight with a competing or completing admonition. Chapters 7 and 10 are filled with these back-and-forth, parrying high jinks, which Qohelet, as present senior rabbi, so to speak, sometimes concludes or absorbs into the aphoristic brief he is intent on making. What looks like a hodgepodge jumble of quotations to an analyst expecting syllogistic order is really a very subtle literary way to show the limits of proverbial knowledge and to suggest that the wisdom of knowing what is "better"—which is serviceable to people seeking guidance—may still fall short of the authentic wisdom that brings flourishing life that is good, rather than allowing people to settle for a praxis of just coping (cf. 7:11-12,15-18,23-24).

Finally, in the last verses of the final chapter, the Holy Spirited editor has the opening line of the book repeated (12:8, 1:2), showing its composed unity as a whole text, and characterizes what Qohelet and wise rabbis always aim to do, namely, goad the congregation populace to walk uprightly and firmly in the Way of truth (12:9-11). And just so nobody can miss the cohering point of the whole complex storied undertaking, the authorial editor has a final chorus of voices exclaiming, "Stand in awe of God and follow God's commandments because God shall eventually sort

1. The careful exegesis of Seow and Bartholomew supports this reading.

out what is genuinely good from what was deceptive and evil" (12:13-14).

So these are the voices in the text you will hear: scribal editor, Qohelet the rabbi, his two younger student rabbi's in training, a choreographed refrain, Woman Wisdom, and several responsive voices edited into the reflective ending of the book.

הבל Strong language

To help you not to be shocked or to take offense I should explain briefly the translation of הבל הבלים which is usually rendered "vanity of vanities," (הבל means "a whiff of (bad) air," "flatulence[2]." The Septuagint translated הבל as ματαιότης "a bombastic emptiness[3]," which the Vulgate turned into *vanitas vanitatum*, a critique of human pretension. "Vanity" has been taken to mean in modern times the affectation of importance men can falsely assume, or the primping of a woman before the mirror in her boudoir. But הבל is worse than human "vanity," and is used throughout the Older Testament to refer to idols, to no-gods, fake deities, worthless puffed-up impotencies[4], which the Bible has no compunction against likening to "passing gas." הבל means "a fart." That's the way the Bible pictures imposters of God—nauseous, gaseous, wasteful vapours like the enveloping choking exhaust which engulfs a pedestrian in the thick of massed idling cars in a traffic jam during rush hour on a clogged Toronto street—"vanity, הבל, going nowhere fast with a stifling Big Stink. Think of Isaiah's inspired ridicule of idols (People cut down a tree, use half of it on which to cook their meal, and pray to the other half as if it be God! 44:1-20). Well, the prologue and epilogue of *Ecclesiastes* uses the superlative, 1:2 12:8 (הבל הבלים). Just as *The Song of Songs* means *The Greatest Song*, so הבל הבלים means, in colloquial English, "The Most Enormous Puff Possible of Stinking Hot Air," condamnably so!

This strong language may make you feel uncomfortable, especially if you are accustomed to having the Bible served up to you soft-boiled, a plum pudding on a Victorian platter, rather than have to eat it like raw fish. But the Qohelet character in *Ecclesiastes*, who has doggedly spent a philosophical lifetime searching existentially for the meaning of things, is utterly frustrated. Not only "wine-women-and-song" (1:12-2:11), but riches, recognition, and a solid, hard-earned legacy achievement (2:12-23)—all these shimmering bubbles have always burst! We men die like animals (3:18-21);

---

2. Buber translates הבל with Dunst, a collective noun, "fumes."
3. Cf. also Ephesians 4:17-19; II Peter 2:17-22, v.18.
4 Cf. Deuteronomy 32:21; I Kings 16:13,26; II Kings 17:15; Psalm 31:6; Jeremiah 2:5, 14:22, 16:19, 23:16.

the healthy-wealthy-and-wise stop breathing as well as those unfortunates mired in poverty or the stupids of the world (5:12-16). What a waste! It's a damn shame! Death is wrong! It's a curse! Everything is really meaningless![5] ... Isn't it?

When I say the Bible is God-speaking literature, you need to take in what I mean. When Lady Macbeth in Shakespeare (*Macbeth* V,1) is trying to wipe out King Duncan's blood from her little, murderous hands, and says, "Out! damned spot—out, I say!" she is not loosely cursing, but agonizing at the crux of a very moral theatre piece in realizing the irretrievable damning guilty evil of her deed. When the prophet Ezekiel, son of a priest called to be spotlessly pure, immaculate, when serving the perfect Holy God with unblemished sacrifices, describes the cheap offerings of God's people and their humdrum adulteries, Ezekiel develops an extremely colourful, refined scatological vocabulary for "whoring" and "sin" (chapter 23:18-20, 36:22-32, I'll not repeat), not to be dirty, but to give vent to the outrage of God who made us men and women innocent creatures without guile, and look what puny, preening filthy hypocrites we have become (*Ecclesiastes* 7:29)!

That is, we need to take Qohelet's exasperated, venting expostulations with a grain of literary salt. Literary language, even when it is God-speaking literary language, revealing God's self—in the lamenting *Psalms*, in the pompous diatribes in the book of Job, in the crass, lustful speeches of Solomon in *The Greatest Song*[6]—one needs, in hearing *Ecclesiastes*, to be ready to listen for exaggerating language, subtle irony, the shift from indicative narrative to speeches with imperatives, the gentle insertion of a subjunctive mood, a tantalizing optative nuance, rhetorical questions, if one wants to hear the actual message literarily booked from God. A closing comment in *Ecclesiastes* 12:12, about how hem-and-haw investigation can wear a person out, does indeed hint that Qohelet's indefatigable searchings may not be the whole story. Still, how seriously we must face what he found to be so—הבל הבלים.

The Counterpoint of Qohelet and the refrain

You see, the refrain in the book of *Ecclesiastes* complements, mit-

---

5   I wonder whether it is more than a coincidence that the first innocent person to be murdered in history, by his older brother Cain, was called "Abel," the exact word in *Ecclesiastes* for "a brief gasp of bad air." The death of Abel was worse than nothing. It was an inexplicable, hateful, damnable curse in God's face. This is precisely what the devout Qoheleth (cf. 6:10-12, 7:29) is saying about the enormous waste of human effort and the despicable injustices he has spent time "finding out" under the sun.

6   Cf. my exposition of *The Song of Songs*, chapter 7:1-9a, in *The Greatest Song in critique of Solomon* (Toronto: Tuppence Press, 2nd ed., 1988), 68-73.

igates, and perforates the buffeted Qohelet's firsthand, darkly-reported observations and deep sustained, relentless questionings and bittersweet reflection. The fact that there is this back-and-forth, teeter-totter shimmy throughout the book in its very fabric, as well as in presentation of different themes, even down to details, is called "wisdom literature." I call it the "Yes, but" rabbinical format for teaching God's Word.[7]

For example, *Proverbs* chapter 1 quotes the swearing come-on of evil men (1:11-14) before it counters the Wisdom Woman speech in the public square proffering the LORD's direction instead (1:22-33). *Proverbs* 7 tells a vivid parable of a prostitute's seducing a young man (7:6-20), before it mentions that he goes like an ox to be slaughtered at the abattoir (7:21-27). Many a biblical psalm chews out God for the believer's being hurt by enemies, until there comes a *waw* adversative turn: "But," I know, God, You shall indeed come through.[8] When you read a chapter of denunciations and impending punishment in Isaiah, a seasoned reader keeps going, because you know a melting chapter of God's forgiving blessing is coming—that's who God is (e.g., 56:9-59:19 followed by 59:20-62:12).

So, to get the point of *Ecclesiastes*, it is critical to grasp the whole literarily composed piece, like a symphony or a well-plotted cinematic production. Yes, Qohelet, life is an enigmatic charade, actually a vulgar bad joke of false promises as the Newer Testament book of James puts it: "You, O man or woman, are just a little misty vapour which appears briefly boasting, and then pfft!, vanishes" (4:13-17)—but, **asks** the refrain, "Have you ever tasted a small piece of freshly baked bread with a glass of good red wine? Or experienced, as Chaucer puts it, the simple, joyful pleasure of working up to a relaxed sweating in the warming sun!?"

As I hear it, the first time the thought of the refrain is broached about suddenly finding joy in one's work and receiving satisfaction from eating and drinking, it is posed as a tentative question: do such basic gifts of ordinary health come occasionally from God's hand? But as the narrative of Qohelet's search for lasting meaning runs into worse roadblocks—seeing rampant violence and jealous, competitive cruelty in society (4:1-6), desperately lonely singles (4:7-12), corrupt governing officials and profiteering

---

7   Cf. Calvin Seerveld, "*Proverbs* 10:1-22: From *Poetic Paragraphs to Preaching, in Reading and Hearing the Word: From Text to Sermon. Essays in Honor of John H. Stek*, ed. Aris C. Leder (Grand Rapids: Calvin Theological Seminary & CRC Publications, 1998), 190-193.

8   In *A Sacred Sorrow, Experience Guide. Reaching Out to God in the Lost Language of Lament* (Colorado Springs: NAV Press, 2005), p.29, Michael Card lists the following: Psalm 3:3, 13:5, 22:19, 41:10, 55:16, 69:13, 71:14, 73:23.

crooks on the make who then go bankrupt (5:7-16)—the refrain wonders
if maybe what God does portion out in our lives is for keeps (3:12-15,22).
When you are overcome by moments of genuine gladness, says the next
refrain, you do not brood about the shortness of your life and that you will
leave it as naked as you entered (5:17-19; cf. Matthew 6:34).

You will notice that in the presentation this evening, I hope, that
as we proceed through the piece, it becomes more buoyant. Not less
hard-hitting, but more tempered, tractable. Qohelet almost stops using
the word הבל—which word has been used almost as often in the first half
of *Ecclesiastes* as in the rest of the Bible—and even stops using his other fa-
vourite phrase: "life is like vainly trying to catch a snatch of wind" (6:9).[9]
And after the first extended display of wise fellows debating proverbs on
what is "better"—"Is a deathdate better than a birthday"? (7:16)—the
fourth refrain introduces this astounding revelation: on good days be
cheerful, and on bad days hang firmly onto this—God is the One in
charge of evil days as well as good days (7:13-14)!

It is very important to understand this declaration rightly in its literary context. You need to hear it like a grown-up little child being told
the truth: you can trust God no matter what happens, because you as a
human creature cannot figure out the amazing deeds of God! That is, the
Bible verse must not be flattened out as if it be a stoical dogmatic statement—God does good and God does evil; so take whatever comes on
the chin. Instead, in the cradle-rocking rhythm of Qohelet's exhausting
search to find out what in God's world is going on, and with the refrain's
pointing to little epiphanies of solid blessing, the fourth time the refrain
appears, it calls attention to the fact that humans are not in charge of all
that happens.

And it is fascinating to watch the Qohelet character change the tone
of his investigation when he admits, "That's right: I found out a lot about
what's relatively better and worse; I put two and two together to thread
my way past pseudo-morality, sexual seduction, and atrocious malevo-
lence, but I could not find Woman Wisdom! I could not figure out myself the sense of Evil and why Life existed!" (7:23-28). And once Qohelet
accepts the matter that as human he cannot be absolutely omniscient and
does not have to be so all-knowing, he becomes less bitter (7:29-8:1).
Qohelet still curses the absurdity of tricky people being honoured and
those with integrity being maligned, but he is comforted by the assurance
that those who stand in awe of God will be cared for and come to rest,
while the wicked remain flitting by like shadows (8:19-14, 8:16-9:1).

---

9. 1:14; 2:11, 17, 26; 4:4; 5:15

Late in the book Qohelet even modifies Death, which he earlier had considered blankly an implacable monstrous הבל 3:16-21: Qohelet now sees human mortality to be an occasion to take responsibility for living life to the hilt while God gives you the opportunity (9:2-6). This judgment chimes in precisely with what the later refrains champion: whatever your hands find to do which God can bless, including a married union, do it with all your might (8:15, 9:8-10)! And the humbled Qohelet comes to admit the limitations of being a trained, proverbial, wise person as he kibitzes on a pyrotechnical display of the two proverb quoters doing their stuff: stupid people in charge may ignore your wisdom; foolish talk may overrule your insights; and debauched rulers may find truth-tellers to be traitors (9:13-10:20). Then, the Woman Wisdom voice comes into her own in the last two chapters (11:1-6; 12:1-7)—the Woman Qohelth could not find (7:28-29)—along with the final seventh refrain (11:7-10). Qohelet's self is moved to align his voice with that of Woman Wisdom, offering a smidgen of hopefulness, that while "the dust turns back to dirt as it once was … the breath of life turns back to God who once gave it" (12:7).

The challenging, steadying Woman Wisdom voice

Think of the Woman Wisdom voice as if she be, I suggested, the hidden, resident, good conscience of Qohelet, which becomes the overpowering, resounding, good Wisdom news at the end of *Ecclesiastes*, comparable to the role God's voice plays at the conclusion of the book of Job. Already in chapter 3, the Wisdom voice picks up the disconsolate prologue intimation that natural processes are just a tiresome ratrace of never-ending, canceling, out-maneuvering (1:4-11), to say, "Not so! God's timing of day and night, ebb and flow, seedtime and harvest, tiny joys amid hard labour and sorrow, are all about God's patient, faithful caring for God's creatures. The sun is not struggling to finish its rounds (cf. 1:5), but is like a bridegroom joyfully rising from its marriage bed each morning" (Psalm 19:4b-6)! Taking a deep breath, able to have a good cry, finding a lost coin, forgetting your friend's anniversary: the press and change of daily life is purely a fascinating gift of the Creator God. And you can count on it, says the consoling Wisdom voice in chapter 3:15; **"God picks up the broken pieces of our lives."** That revelation alone is worth the whole book of *Ecclesiastes*.

The Wisdom voice speaks the first imperative in the book of *Ecclesiastes* (Hebrew 4:17- 5:5, English/Spanish 5:1-6): "Don't talk so much when you go to God's house and make easy promises; God is in heaven and you are on the earth; so watch out, listen quietly in awe." I find it significant that the Wisdom voice does not silence the coarse-speaking Qohelet, who is struggling out in the boisterous tumult of the street, but cautions the decent people who go worship and talk nicely with God. This vignette in *Ecclesiastes* reminds me of Isaiah chapter 1:10-20, where God tells worshippers to stop bringing God offerings like presents, while there you do nothing to rescue the derelict, the poor, and victims of injustice that makes me puke, says God. Maybe you remember too the parable Jesus told, which reinforces this *Ecclesiastes* passage in chapter 5, about the smooth-talking Pharisee and the abject Publican, who dared only utter, "Lord, be merciful to me, a sinner" (Luke 18:9-14). It is wise, says the Bible, not to talk too much, especially if you want to be "genuine" as a person in God's world.

Wisdom's next speech comes right after the turning point in the book, when Qohelet humbly owns up to it that the only thing he "figured out" (מצאתי) is that God created humans upright, but what devious creatures we have become (7:26-29; cf. 7:14,24 and 8:17)! The Wisdom voice bookends Qohelet's admission by saying that a deeply perceptive, wise person knows that evil will get its comeuppance—evil doers are haunted by restlessness—but do not presume that you yourself must set it right straightaway—plotted evil can exceed human power (8:2-8). So be circumspect, says Lady Wisdom still later, remembering that God is in the picture, yet fervently give away your gifts indiscriminately without trying to gauge the prospects of success in a world so overrun by wrongs (11:1-6). Wisdom, with the final refrain, sounds very close to the Newer Testament exhortation, "Always be glad in the Lord; let your forbearance (τὸ ἐπιεικὲς) be known to everybody (because) the Lord is nearby. Let God's peace-giving end any deep deep uncertainty and anxiety" (Philippians 4:4-7).

The explorations of the chastened Qohelet, the fireworks of proverb-quoting fellows who know what is "better," and the refrain that grows in telling with assurance that the simple pleasures of daily sustenance of work, bread and wine are occasions for joyful thanksgiving, all culminate in the final refrain and Wisdom's last apocalyptic, poetic, imperative speech. The call to enjoy life is very Semitic, not particularly evangelical. However, Wisdom and the refrain have a robust conviction that God's creation is a rich source of blessing and joy, especially if you are mindful of God's timing. You personally cannot always figure that out—God's timing—says Wisdom in chapter 3:11, but you can enjoy the strength of your youth, Wisdom encourages in the final refrain: the red blood coursing through your veins, the growing beard, the developing breasts; revel in the engaging curiosities everywhere (11:9-10). Yes, says Wisdom, get close to the Creator, you young folk, before you are past such flourishing times and have creaky knees, which make you say, "I don't really feel like it" (12:1).

In fact, says the Wisdom voice to old and young, you need to learn to recognize your Creator before the sun and moon and stars turn dark, before what's up in the air makes even strong men double up afraid. Become intimate with the Creator God before the night comes when people can no longer work (cf. John 4, especially v.4), before the birds and the grasshoppers and the trees start to wilt and peter out. Get close to your Creator God before artworks of gold and silver will be smashed to bits, before water on which life depends is made unavailable! That is, listen closely to God, snuggle into God's arms, before the Final apocalyptic Day of reckoning with God on good and evil comes, so that you be not dead before the time when God receives back the life-breath God gave you (12:2-7).

If you do not experience the goodness of creation, do not recognize the excitement of puberty, the wonder of sunlight, the blessing of hard work in which you can give your very self away as a thank-offering to God and neighbour—if you do not experience daily troubled life as activity brimming over with God's justifying mercy—you are dead to the world, says *Ecclesiastes*. You walk around like a zombie on earth if you do not live life holding hands with the Creator God. You are not genuinely human. Death is like spilled milk. Well, human life that is all talk-talk-talk, thought-thought-writing books, scrambling for possessions, power and prestige, but acting as if you are without a Creator makes you a counterfeit, a dead man walking, in a word, הכל.

Historical setting, literary cast, Lady Wisdom as Holy Spirit

So, I've walked you through the biblical book of *Ecclesiastes* and prepared you somewhat for the live presentation this evening of God speaking through a chorus of voices. Let me add just a note about its historical setting and mention once more the educated literary quality of the composition of the book; and then tie its Wisdom format into the rest of the Bible story.

Ecclesiastes was probably booked c.350 BC, when Persian King Ochus Artaxerxes and his generals were fighting against the disintegration of their worldly empire. Israel as a nation in the buffer military zone nearby was in a mess. *Ecclesiastes* notes corruption at large in both the legal system and the temple organization (3:16, 4:1, 5:8, 10:5-7). The Jewish leadership at this time had such a defensive mentality that they had set up a theocracy in Jerusalem! So the climactic good news of Wisdom to throw your bread freely out upon the surrounding waters would have sounded to God's people then like stark-raving madness.

Many scholars of *Ecclesiastes* have found it to be a chorus (better, a cacophony) of voices, but agree that the careful avoidance of Solomon's name anywhere (cf. 1:12-2:23) means Solomon was not used by the Holy Spirit as author.[10] The fact that *Ecclesiastes* is chuck-full of proverbs, and a closing voice uses the standard term 12:12 (בני, "my good fellows"), which a Qohelet uses for catechizing learners, situates the text firmly in the so-called "wisdom literature" writings of the Bible. My contribution for someone's understanding the book is to show its unity of style and edited authorial composition (the important change in Qohelet), the presence of the sevenfold refrain on joyful acceptance of Creator God's gifts, and especially my recognition of the voice of Woman Wisdom, which is in tune with the tradition in the book of Proverbs 1-9.

It is critical, I think, to take seriously the literary nature of the text. *Ecclesiastes* is not a categorical treatise, it is God's Word given in a parabolic, story-telling, almost Noh-theatre allusive format of placed voices. So the final "statement," spoken by the chorus of voices responding to the main body of the book—**"Stand in awe of God and keep God's commandments"**—is not to be heard as a dogmatic command you have to logically agree with, so much as a cheer! It is a winsome witness by those who have survived the journey through this intense melee of point-and-counterpoint thrusts of questions and struggle to know the truth about the meaning of things. If you want to join in with the cheer,

---

10 In 1968 Addison Wright summarized the many early modern commentators who found the book of *Ecclesiastes* to be without any discernible unifying structure (e.g., F. Delitsch 1891, G. Wildeboer 1898, A.H. McNeile 1904, G.A. Barton 1908, A.L Williams 1922, G. Kuhn 1926, B. Gemser 1931, K. Galling 1932, E.H. Pfeiffer 1932, R. Gordis 1955, W. Zimmerli 1962, H.W. Hertzberg 1963, O Eissfeldt 1965, R.B.Y. Scott 1965), while Wright himself contended that *Ecclesiastes* had a carefully composed order (1968, 314). Wright reaffirmed his thesis twelve years later (1980). In the meantime Michael Fox had proposed that *Ecclesiastes* is a well-integrated composition (1977). Choon-Leong Seow in his 1997 Anchor Bible commentary on *Ecclesiastes* (46) hedges a bit but, following and modifying F.J. Backhaus in *Denn Zeit und Zufall trifft sie alle* (Frankfurt am Main: Anton Hain, 1993), affirms that there be, "on formal, semantic, and contextual grounds," four coherent compositions in the book: (IA) 1:2-4:16; (IB) 5:1-6:9; (IIA) 6:10-8:17, (IIB) 9:1-12:8. Reformational philosopher K.J. Popma's judgment was " ... het boek *Prediker* een verslag is van een discussie waaraan vele en in overtuiging uiteenlopende sprekers deelnamen ... " (1961, 4).

good for you—that's the sidewise, winsome appeal of God's call for you to become "genuine," honest to God.

If you read *Ecclesiastes* carefully, together with other books of the Bible, I believe you will discover that the voice of capital "W" Woman Wisdom is an alias for God the Holy Spirit (just as Woman Foolishness is a stand-in for Σάρξ (cf. Proverbs 9). In the speech by Wisdom in *Proverbs* 1:20-33, Wisdom says explicitly, "I will pour out my Spirit (רוּחִי upon you" (1:23). In the speech by Wisdom in Proverbs 8:1-36, Wisdom talks about her presence with God before creation of the world (8:22-31), precisely the way Genesis 1:1-2 talks about the Spirit of God hovering over the face of the formless waters. Exodus 31:1-11 credits the Spirit of God for filling the tabernacle artisans Bezaeel and Oholiab with their "wisdom, understanding, inside knowledge of all kinds of craft ability" (31:3). The Babylonian Queen of King Belshazzar announces that Daniel is the godly, wise man needed because "the Spirit of the holy gods" is in him (Daniel 5:10-12). And Isaiah prophesies about the coming Messiah, that "the Spirit of the LORD God, that is, the Spirit of Wisdom, insight, wise counsel, power, the Spirit of intimate knowledge and awe of the LORD will rest upon him" (Isaiah 11:2), and the writers of the Newer Testament gospels according to Mark and John attest that this indeed happened at the baptism of Jesus Christ when the Holy Spirit descended upon him (Mark 1:9-13, John 1:29-34).

That Lady Wisdom metaphorically represents the Holy Spirit God helps us understand why Qohelet's search to "figure out" what was "wise" fractured, and why his countenance softened once he began to realize that true Wisdom is the gift of the Spirit, to stand in awe (5:16, 7:18), to trust God, whose everlasting provident care of everyone's "portion" (חלק) is "wise" and sure (3:10-15, 5:17-18). The Wisdom voice of *Ecclesiastes* is a profound rejection of the faith in human rational intelligence to figure out solutions for our world's historical troubles, and a strong encouragement to keep the quality of lasting joy in transient pleasure.

I mean this: (1) It is foolish, according to *Ecclesiastes*, to try to "figure out" Evil and justify the ways of God to man. Theodicy proudly overstates the limits of human knowledge (8:16-17). Holy-Spirited wisdom, on the other hand, tries selflessly to give away merciful justice to all and sundry, and be content to rest in laments and hymns of praise, as do the biblical psalms.

(2) When the pleasure of enjoying the fruits of one's labours, tasting in peace with friends the wine of God's vineyard, sitting in the shade of your fig tree (cf. Micah 4:4, Zechariah 3:10)—when such pleasure bears

the holy coefficient of God-thanking joy, such moments will be saved forever (3:12-14)! When one's pleasures are stripped of eschatonic joy and become bare self-indulgent sensations, however, God's good creatural gift of enjoyment is short-circuited and leaves a bitter aftertaste (7:26), because such cravings remain at heart mean and godless (cf. Romans 14:17, Titus 3:3). But it is possible even to go through persecution with confident cheer, says the Bible, convinced against all odds that God will pick up the pieces (3:15, Hebrews 10:32-39), and that a restorative feast is in the offing (Isaiah 60, Revelation 19).

God does really pick up the broken pieces of our lives, individually and communally in history, of those who become adopted children of God and even of those who are still living illegitimately on their own borrowed time (Hebrew 12:1-11). It is true to *Ecclesiastes* to think of God as patrolling the city streets nights, the terrible stretches of war zones, **and** the "normal" suburban neighbourhoods, where hateful human cruelty, both open and concealed, is occurring daily, leaving broken, desolate victims behind: God, the softly crying Garbage Collector, is busy picking up what's left over of our human, selfish, self-righteous, greedy, and bloody deeds. So, hear the biblical text call out to you, and believe: God does pick up the pieces! and does that often through the compassionate acts toward others by the community of those who follow Jesus, not expecting rewards, but just for the joy of it (Matthew 25:31-46, I Peter 2:21, Hebrews 12:12-14)!

Remember the *Ecclesiastes* toast: **Stand in awe of God and keep God's commandments** (*Ecclesiastes* 12:13)! **Amid your tears, cheers!** That is what it means, according to the book of *Ecclesiastes*, to be an "authentic" human creature in God's world being saved by Jesus Christ.

Egyptian Coptic Woman c. 1950s

I imagine the Woman Wisdom voice comes from a mature woman of colour. Voice pitch is contralto, and the intonation is a cross between that of Deborah, Naomi, and Esther. She provides the comforting firm gentleness of the Holy Spirit.

3

A LITERARY TRANSLATION OF *ECCLESIASTES*: GOD'S WORDS OF QOHELET AND OTHERS*

VOICES:

E Editor/author, **Q** Qohelet, **W** Woman Wisdom, **R1** Young apprentice rabbi, **R2** Young apprentice rabbi, **Refr** Sevenfold refrain.

1:2-1:8 **E**   Stinking hot air! Utter Nonsense! says Qohelet.
        It's all just a big fart!
    What's a person got left after all his or her hard work,
        a person who does their damned best on this earth?
        What's left?!
    The earth stays put forever,
        but a generation of men and women goes when
        an other generation comes (onto the scene).
    The sun too rises up shining only to fall down,
        hard pressed in fact to get back to the place
        where it must start over again.
    And the wind blustering to the South,
        then fluttering back to the North, circling this way
        that away always crisscross doubling back and forth
        on itself ... so tosses the wind.
    All the rivers flow into the sea,
        yet the sea never gets full;
        so there the rivers go, flowing, flowing, flowing to
        the place where they always unfilling flow....
    Everything, I tell you, every blasted thing—
        a person can't begin to relate them all;
        no eye finishes seeing, no ear finishes hearing it all
        —every thing is everlastingly,
        exhaustedly busy moving ... (where to)?

*Parentheses in the translated text are my additions to clarify what the original text phrase implied.

1:9-1:17   What has been will be again, and
           what happened in the past will happen again:
           there is nothing new going on under the sun.

           Or is there something you could say: "Look at this!
              something genuinely new!"
           Nah. It was there already long ago, before our time.
           People today just ignore learning about earlier things.
           Things that are still to happen will not be remembered
              either by the people who come after those things.

Q   Look, I'm a philosopher.
           Once upon a time there was a king of Israel in Jerusalem....

           And I thought to myself, how about looking into things
              to find out by wisdom what the sense is to all that's
              being done under the heavens—it's a bad business,
              a back-breaking business God has pressed down
              upon the human race.
           So I took a careful look at all the doings going on night
              and day under the sun; and you know—it's all a bad
              joke, like chasing wind!

R1   "What's once been crooked,
              nobody can ever make entirely straight."
Q   And what's not there, you can't figure out somehow.

           I prided myself, I did, thinking out loud, "Do you see
              how significantly you have developed experiential
              knowledge beyond anything ever thought out before
              you in Jerusalem?"
           And I had, I really had come to grips with a tremendous
              deal of knowledge and enriching experience.
           I was determined to not only be familiar with what
              makes sense and is valuable but also to know
              intimately all kinds of mad foolishness
              and outright stupidity.
           I gradually learned, though, that even such endeavour
              is chasing wisps of wind.

1:18-2:8

    R2   "Much wisdom brings with it much irritable
                 sensitivity."

    Q   And greater insight only means greater heartache.

I said to myself, All right then, go ahead, let me try it
    out, eating, drinking, making merry—saturating
    yourself with what's pleasant—but it was no use.
That's right! The pleasant passed with a brief breath.
Good old belly laughs, I had to admit, how crazy!
    And the song-and-dance flirt,
      what does it really do?
I deliberately figured out how to stimulate the senses,
    prickle the body with wine, while keeping my head
    clear enough to reflect thoughtfully.
I skillfully learned to grab hold of what is
    respectably foolish, live it until I could tell:
    is this now good for the run of men and women to
    do under heaven for the so few days of their life?
I began to do "big" things! I built me palatial houses.
    I had mountain side vineyards laid out and
    cultivated for myself.
I made me gardens and forest paradises planted full
    with all kinds of blossoming fruit trees.
I constructed artificial lakes for myself, reservoirs, to
    irrigate the parks literally chock-full of thirstily
    growing trees.
I bought me male slaves and female slaves and had baby
    slaves born in my household.
I naturally acquired vast herds of cattle, sheep and
    goats. I got me much, much more than anyone
    before me had in Jerusalem.
I collected—yes, I became a collector!—of silver and gold;
    I brought together for myself treasures of kings
    and the tribute of satrapies.
I got me male choirs and female choirs.
I surrounded myself with the titillating delight of
    all men everywhere: women, I mean "Busty
    Women!"—noble ladies, gentlewomen,
    maids and wenches.

2:9-2:16   So I became important. I piled up more riches than
            anyone who ever lived before me in Jerusalem;
            yet on top of all that I kept my head!
            I kept my investigating presence of mind.

            Nothing that fascinated my eyes did I turn away from.
            I did not at heart hold back from any pleasure, and
            I really was enjoying myself through the whole
            gamut of exertions—that was my reward, I guess,
            for all the trouble.
            But when I stopped, half-turned to evaluate all the
            products my very own hands had produced—when
            I took stock, pondered the terribly hard effort that
            had gone into accomplishing what I had stuck to
            toiling at—I could have....
            It was all a mirage! I had been chasing the wind!
            There would be nothing left over!
            Nothing would remain under the sun.

            I continued probing to get at what's wise and to know
            what's fool-headed and asinine from the inside,
            because otherwise what would happen to the
            person who comes along afterward and tries to
            do exactly what the king did?
            I noticed, of course, that being wise had advantages over
            being foolish, just as light helps more than darkness—

R1   "The wise have eyes in their head,
            while a fool stumbles around in the dark."

Q   but both wise person and fool—I know firsthand
            what I'm talking about!—the same blasted thing
            hits them both!

            Do you realize, I thought to myself, that what happens
            to the fool is going to happen to you too? And so
            what! I was so very very wise once upon a time.
            So I realized, under my breath, that wisdom too is
            a sometime thing: there is no more extended
            celebrative memory of a wise person than a

2:16-2:25   fool: both are forgotten practically before they are
                    known—it's a pitiable fact! The philosopher like his
                    fellow fool ends up dead!

                 About then I had enough; what the hell—It struck me
                    evil, all the straining work sweated out on the earth,
                    because it's all stinking worthless! Wind-chasing!
                 I hated the whole business! Everything I had carefully,
                    laboriously struggled for under the sun I hated,
                    because (I knew) I had to leave it to somebody else
                    coming along later, and who knows
                    whether that person will be sensible or a fellow who
                    couldn't care less? But no matter which—that person
                    gets it! That person shall dispose of the whole works,
                    everything I slaved for, trying to be wise under the
                    sun. There it goes—pfftt!
                 This is why, cringing deep inside, I dejectedly
                    gave up expecting anything from all my hard work
                    on this earth. If a person toils intelligently,
                    prudently, ably, only to drop it in the lap of a man
                    who doesn't work for it at all—it's all yours!—
                    what kind of farce is that? Right! It's a monstrous
                    curse!
                 What does a man or woman get out of it? All this honest
                    labour, this conscientious striving to sweat it out
                    here below, every day an endurance, this work a
                    nagging tension so that even nights you can't quietly
                    sleep—is that not a cursed stupidity? Total nonsense?!

Refr1   **Is then the best thing (possible) with a man or a
             woman that they just eat and drink and become one
             who surprises oneself at finding joy in the job for the
             day? (No! That can't be it ... can it?)**

Q   Besides, I clearly saw that even such simple joys come only
                    out of God's hand.

Refr1   **For who can eat, who can relish (anything)
                    apart from God?**

2:26-3:9   **It is God who gives wisdom, insight, and joy to a man**
                     or a woman,
              one who pleases God.
              But to whoever remains thanklessly cold,

              God gives the trouble of collecting and stacking things
              up—so that God may give it away to someone
                     who is lovely in the eye of God!

Q   So, (craving) simple joys is also misplaced activity,
             a useless chase of hot air?

W   There is a right time for everything, is there not?
             There seems to be time
                 for every kind of activity under the sun:
                 time to give birth and time to die,
                 time for planting, time for weeding out
                    what was planted,
                 a time to kill and a time to heal,
                 time to break down and time to build up,
                 time to weep and time to laugh,
                 a time of mourning, and a time of dancing around,
                 time to throw stones and time to pick up stones,
                 a time for embracing, and a time to keep yourself far
                 away from embracing;
             (There seems to be)
                 a time to struggle for something,
                 and a time to give it up as lost,
                 time to save things, and time to throw away things,
                 time to tear things to pieces,
                 and time to sew things together,
                 a time to keep quiet and a time to speak out,
                 time to love, time to hate,
                 a time of close infighting,
                 and a time of being at peace...
             What's the use?
             What is left over of the labour to which a man or a
                 woman exerts oneself?!

3:10-3:19 I have come to see through this miserable problem
which God has given humans to bother them:
Everything God has ever done is very good,
  done at the right time;
this timing—eternity—God has put
  at the heart of humans too
(this does not mean humans can find out what God
actually has been doing from beginning to end).

Ref2 **I have come to understand that men and women can
  do nothing good themselves,
that for a man or woman to be glad, to be well-off in
  their lives,
for any person even to be able to eat
  and drink and enjoy themselves
  in the constant press and change of daily life,
all this is purely a gift of God!
I have come to understand experientially that
whatever God does lasts forever –
nothing can be added to it and nothing can be taken
  away from it.
God has set things up this way so that humans
  will stand in awe before God's presence.
Whatever is and will be has already been:
God picks up the pieces!**

Q But when I went outside again to see what I could see
  under the sun, I saw in the place for
  administering justice injustice executed;
  instead of declarations there declaring what is right,
I saw practised a killing pseudo-justice!
The old thought came to me, "God shall (someday)
  pronounce judgment on the just and the unjust"—
  everything, every deed has its day coming.
But probing deeper I told myself: this is God's way to
  pinpoint for the sons and daughters of man,
  push them to recognize, that so far as humans can
  tell, they are no more, than animals.
What happens to the beast befalls humankind,
  the same thing—one dies like the other,

3:19-4:5   both breathe the same; a human
                   has no superiority to an animal on that score;
                   both are a little gasp of escaping hot air.
                   They both end up in the same place:
                        from dust they came,
                   to dust they both disintegrate—
               (or) did someone ever notice the life breath
               of humans rising up somewhere, and watch
               breath of animals sinking down,
                        down to the ground?
               So firsthand experience still left me wondering.

W   **Since no one lives to see what happens
           after he or she expires,
       is there anything better for a man or woman than
       that they joy in what they are doing?
       At least that is allotted them, if it is ...**

Q   Wherever I turned I saw the violence,
           all the cruel, deceptive,
           oppressive acts committed under the sun.
       And I watched—Oh, my!—tears of the violated drop.
       No one was comforting them, forcibly beaten,
           raped by the strong hand of those brutalizing
           them—there was no one comforting them!
       Happy are the dead, I said, those already dead,
           rather than these alive,
           these who are still breathing;
           and better than either are the unborn
           who have not had to live through the ugly evil
           going on under the sun.
       All the effort at work and all the hard-won success
           at managing things,
       I saw that too; and I saw it was (simply) jealous man
           or woman trying to get ahead of their neighbour.
       How can you be so stupid, trying to negotiate a fart?

R2   They say, "It is a fool who folds his hands
       and whiles himself away to death."

4:6-4:15

Q   But is it not "Better to have a handful of rest
than both fists balled, punching the empty wind?"

So I kept on going back to study the endless struggles
taking place under the sun ...
There was the single person who (decided to) go it alone,
no child, rid of relatives, one who slaved
indefatigably, eyes never tiring of watching
more money (come in).
But "who am I killing myself for, denying myself
every pleasure?"
Independence too is an overrated dream, a tormented
undertaking.

R1   "Two people together are better off than one alone."
Q   With two is at least the reassuring good
in their troubled, workaday life that if they fall,
the one will get the other fellow up; but too
bad for the loner if he or she fall,
for there is no second one around
to help the other up again.
And if two lie down together to sleep,
they can be warm; but how can the single,
lonely one get warm?
Though someone overpower the person
who goes it alone,
two together shall stand up to the attack.
R2   "A braided rope is not so quickly broken."

Q   A young man poor but wise is better off
than an established king who
like a fool no longer knows how to take advice:
the youth though born needy, can move,
during that king's reign, from a destitute,
out-of-the-way house up to royal rule—
In fact, I saw it, and I saw every living creature
under the sun trooping along
with the fine young man who would take
the first king's place!

4:16-5:7   You couldn't count all the people,
        all those who crowded behind the new
        successor. But the people who came later on,
       they did not think the second king was so good…
        Rags to riches, gaining political power too,
        is a bubble that bursts, like a constipated fart.

W   You (believers), look out when you go walk into
        the house of God—
     step in, come near to listen,
       rather than bullheaded making it a fool's habit
       of bringing sacrifices,
       doing wrong without knowing it.
     Do not be in such a rush (to use) your mouth;
     don't get all bothered at heart,
       anxious to push your talk
       in front of God's face.
     God is in heaven(!) and you are on the earth;
       so let your words be few.

R1   "Like many tensed activities generate dreams,
       many words mean idle talk, the voice of a fool."

W   If you ever make a vow to God,
       do not dillydally in keeping it:
       God does not think easy promises are funny.
       A vow made must be carried out.
R1   "It is better not to vow than to vow
       and leave it undone."

W   Do not let your mouth drag you bodily
       into a tangle of guilt,
       and then tell God's representative,
       "Oh, it was just a slip of the lips":
     do you want God provoked at your speech?
     Are you egging God on so that God has to let the
       work of your hands miscarry?!

R1   "Like the untold number of dreams,
       there are the millions of utterly empty hot-air words."

5:7-5:15

W   You, instead, **stand in awe of God!**

Q   (As I was saying…)
             When you see it is those without defence
                   that are the ones violated,
                      when you see how justice and what's simply right
                   is subverted throughout the countryside,
                   do not be surprised at this business.
             Above one corrupt official
                   is another profiteering crook,
                   and superior to them still more—
                   what an advantage for a country if,
                   instead of all this, its ruling king lives (simply)
                   from cultivating the land.

R1   "Whoever loves money is not satisfied with money."
R2   "Whoever loves spending money
                   never makes enough profit."
Q   All that too is a rat-race.
R1   "Whenever goods increase, so do the consumers."

Q   So what's the owner getting out of it except watching
             (the economy) flow?

             Sweet is the sleep of a hard-working man or woman
             whether they have eaten a lot or just enough;
             but the overflowing plenty of one who is well-off
             does not allow him or her rest for sleeping.

             That's a disturbing trouble I noticed throughout
                   the earth, how hoarding wealth works
                      to hurt its owner.
             I saw great riches disappear through a misadventure,
             and the fellow had absolutely nothing left
                   in his hand for a child that was born.
             As naked as he came out of his mother's womb,
             just so naked he moved on again,
                   unable to hold on to anything
                   that he could pass on from his hand

5:16–6:2   despite all his concentrated enterprise—
                such a bitter pill it makes you sick!
           Just as you came, just so you go
                (with nothing to hand on to the next generation):
                what good do you get out of it that one strained
                oneself in hard labour for a puff of wind?
           Why, such a fellow ate grudgingly every day of his life,
           eternally discontented, sickly
                and full of gripes to boot—
                (what good does one get out of it all!)

Refr3   **I'm telling you, the one good thing I saw,**
                a wonderful good!
           is eating, drinking, finding joy
                inside all the miserably hard work
           a person sweats at daily under the sun
                for the so few days of life God gives him or her.
           It's a wonderful good allotted that person—
           I mean this:
           whatever money or possession God has given a man
           or woman, every person who is enabled—
                this is God's giving!—enabled to eat from it,
           enabled to freely, fully, actively receive what God has
                specially portioned out for him or her,
                who is enabled to be genuinely happy
                in one's sin-cursed labouring—
           That is a wonderful good!, the one good thing I saw,
           because then a man or a woman does not cumber
                oneself so much brooding over the meagre span
                of one's lifetime:
           God keeps the person preoccupied with a heart
                full of gladness!

Q   It is really an evil thing. It weighed one down.
           I saw it everywhere throughout the earth,
                how a human whom God has given
                financial success, affluence, even an honoured
                reputation, who had everything for himself he
                wanted, not a thing missing! I saw how God,
                nevertheless, did not make him able

6:2-6:10   to partake of it himself—
     a complete stranger ate it up!
     A woeful, flagrantly empty pernicious bitterness.
    If a person gives birth to a hundred children
     and lives for a slew of years, and becomes truly as
     distinguished as his days are long,
      but fails to taste satisfaction himself from all that
     good, and there not even be a burial for him,
     believe me: the stillborn child is better off than he.
    From nowhere to obscurity comes and goes
     that (lump of flesh), bereft of a name,
     unaware of sunlight, void of consciousness:
     but the stillborn babe, not the respected man,
     had rest. Even if he lived a thousand years twice
     over, if a man is unable to be actually glad
     in the good, so what?
    Do not all end up in the same hole?
    All that person's troublesome toil
     was meant for his own mouth, but it missed!
    That which drove him on did not get gratified!
    What advantage would a wise person have
     over the foolish one?
    What does a lowly, suffering man or woman
     know for keeping one's daily life going
     (in contrast to those who live so well off)?
    That they thoroughly know at least this?
    "Present enjoyment of what's visible is better
    than a blood-racing, omnivorous desire?"

    (But is not such common current fascination
     with the present also)
     an insolent bluff, a foolish chase,
     trying to catch the foul wind … ?
    That the human long, long ago was called into being
     a human, and that it was established long,
     long ago that a human is only human,
     and no match for contending with
     the One-who-is-stronger than a human:
     that is what is so.

6:11-7:8   That humans can spew words and multiply deeds
                    only adds up to so much more claptrap:
            who really knows what's good for a human
                    in the so few days of one's lifetime,
                        this damn life which a person vanishes through
                    like a shadow? Because who can tell a person
                    what shall follow up him or her under the sun?

Q   (Do you know what is "good" for us humans?)
R1   "A good reputation is still better
                    than banqueting relaxation."
R2   But "Is a death-date still better than a birthday?"
Q   Yes! Entering a home touched by grief is still better
                    than walking into a house toasting champagne,
            because death is the conclusion of every man
                    and woman, and when the living (face it),
            they have to take it to heart.

R1   "Touchiness is better than a boisterous demeanor."
R2   Right! "Because under a troubled countenance
                    can throb a composed heart."

Q   So, the wise will feel at home where there is sorrow,
            and stupid people lose their hearts in halls of amusement.

R1   It may be so that
                    "It is better to listen to a wise person cursing
                        than stand there to hear the singing of fools,"
R2   because "like the sound of crackling nettles
                    under boiling kettles is the cackling laughter of a fool."
Q   But! cannot talk of the wise also be
                    sugar-coated nonsense?
            For blackmail can reduce a wise person
                    to shameful things; and a gift under the table
                    corrupts the wise person's heart (too).

R2   It's true, "The completion of something
                    is better than its beginning,"
R1   but remember, "It is better to have a forbearing spirit
                    than to show an overbearing attitude."

7:9-7:18

Q   So, do not be so spitfire ready to breathe irritation;
     a worrisome irritability lodges in the belly of fools.
   Do not be constantly saying,
     "Why were the old days better than these days,"
     because such a demand is stupid!

   "Wisdom" (knowing this is better than that) like
     an inheritance is "good,"
     worth having for one who still lives
     with the burning sun,
     because like money
     (such) wisdom affords protective shade.
   Still more worth knowing, however,
     is that (true) Wisdom gives life
     to the one who has (genuine) wisdom!
   I mean this:

Refr4 **Stand amazed at the mighty workings of God!**
    Who could indeed make straight
    what God makes crooked!
    On good days be cheerful, and on bad days
     hang firmly onto this:
    God is the One who makes evil days too,
     as well as good days—
    this is why humans can not find out, determine
     themselves, anything of what follows them—

Q   I've seen both, I tell you, in this damn life of mine:
     a man who acts straight, ruined by his
     righteousness, and a man who deals
     crookedly, thrive long on his underhandedness.
   So don't try to be overly righteous or show yourself off
     as excessively wise—
     are you aching to be finished off—?
     anymore than you would dare to be a
     gross pervert and play the wicked, stupid fool.
     Why die before it's your time?
   It would be "good," all right,
     if you should consistently avoid evil doing,

7:18-7:26   and at the same time also refrain from do-gooding:
            whoever stands in awe of God escapes them both.

R1   "Wisdom," they say, "gives a wise man more strength
           than having ten strong men living in a city."
Q   But no man on earth is so righteous
           he does good without sinning.

R2   "Don't pay close attention to all the word
           and words (people say); you might hear your own
           servant despising you."
Q   Right again, because you know deep down
           in your heart that frequently you too have idly cut
           other people down.

        ... All these kinds of proverbial sayings and the
           well-meant as well as evilly-meant human actions,
           I checked them all out with **a deliberating wisdom**.
           I said again and again, "Let me become **truly wise!**"
           But it everlastingly eluded my grasp....
           Deep, impenetrably hidden is the meaning of things.
           Deep! mysteriously unfathomable
           is the meaning of all that happens.
        Who shall ever be able to figure it out?

        Still, I persisted, busying myself to get inside
           knowledge, to explore in depth,
           to pick my way carefully through clever
           human maneuvers as well as matters of wisdom;
           and I made a point to get to know firsthand
           the malice of intractable impertinence and the
           downright stupidity of godless infatuation.
        For example, I "found out" what the Woman is like
           whose wiles are a fishing net-like labyrinth set
           to catch prey, what fetters her fascinating hands make!
           The one who pleases God shall escape from her, but
           whoever likes to play with sin shall stay caught—
           it is a trap more bitter than death.

7:27-8:7

E   "You see, that is what I found out,"
        says philosopher Qohelet, who put two and two
        together to (try to) figure out (human) invention.

Q   In threading my way deliberately
        (through good and evil), what I could not find—
        I did find one sound person in a thousand—
        in all those detective searches I never found
        Woman (Wisdom)!
    So only this—note well!—did I "figure out":
        God made the human person simple, upright.
    But look at them! They devise untold strategies....

E   Who would be like the truly "wise" person?
    Who really knows thoroughly how to interpret
        the meaning of things?
    A person with true wisdom has one's whole
        bearing in life altered—one's face lightened;
        embittered, hardened features of one's character
            take on a softer, steadying glow.

W   I (too agree): "Do what a king commands."
        Do it because of your oath before God
        (to obey the ruler). Then you need not be afraid
        in the ruler's presence. Leave!
        Do not stand around where evil is hatched,
        because a king does whatever the king wants;
        nobody ever asks a royal ruler,
        "Are you going to do that?"

R1   It could be that "Whoever obeys a command
        never gets into trouble."
W   but (more to the point is what) a deeply perceptive,
    wise person knows: "there comes a time
        for just comeuppance (to evil)."
    Every affair has a time of just comeuppance.
        That is why evil a person has done rests so heavily
        upon him or her—you don't know exactly
        what is going to happen to you, for who could tell

8:7-8:14   you what shall take place?
                   No human controls the wind to box it in.
                   No human has power to determine
                        the day of one's death.
                   Nobody can (by oneself) effect a pause in war.
                   Evil done lets no human who committed it run from the
                        results and escape.

Q   ... I kept on noticing all this kind of thing.
                        I took to heart all that was doing
                        and going on under the sun so long as
                        one man or woman lorded it over
                        another person to hurt them.
                   And on top of that, I saw evil, tricky men getting
                        a funeral burial and resting in peace,
                        while those who did what was proper
                        were driven from the holy place and utterly
                        forgotten in some one or other city—
                        it was a dirty shame!
                   Because judgment is not immediately executed
                        upon wrongdoing, people grow bolder to
                        commit evil. Why, a hardened sinner
                        can do evil a hundred times
                        and still live a long life.
                   Nevertheless, I know certainly
                        that it shall go well with the person
                        who stands in awe of God, who lives awed by
                        God's presence; and it shall not go well
                        with the wicked man or woman—their days
                        shall not last long—that person (exists) like a shadow
                        because he or she does not stand in
                        awe of God's presence.
                   There is a monstrously confusing phenomenon
                        happening on the face of the earth:
                        people of just integrity get what's coming
                   to godless, crooked fellows, and the
                        crooked-dealing persons get what's coming
                        to just-doing men and women.
                   Absurd! I said it again and again—it's a damn shame!

8:15-9:2

Refr5 **So I had good words for any contented joy:**
there is nothing better for a man and a woman
under the sun than eating, drinking and being glad!
And let them cling to it (when it appears)
in this troubled labour for however many days God
has given to each one under the sun.

Q   While I spent my deepest energy to dig out
            what would be "wisdom,"
            and to observe thoroughly the moil wrung
            (from humans) upon earth,
            I came to realize that nobody ever—
            not even if one did not shut his
            or her eyes to sleep night or day—
            can ever find out all that God is doing;
            a person simply cannot figure out
            all the happenings going on under the sun.
            Though a person strain to pick it through
            piece by piece, nobody can ever get
            to the bottom of it all. Even if the "wise person"
            says he or she is about to discover (what's up),
            they cannot at all have figured it out.
      It is so: I took everything to heart
            (—every shred of knowledge and experience
            painstakingly unearthed by the investigation—),
            and this much I got clear, that the tried-and-true folk
            and the wise and all their on-going deeds
            rest in the hand of God. No human alive can know
            whether love or hate shall fall his or her way—
            everything is still ahead of them.

R2   "Every possible thing for every sundry body."

Q   There is one same matter (however) that waits
            for both those of a just-doing integrity
            and for the godless guilty, for the good and pure, and
            for the dirtied impure, for those who
            religiously make sacrifices and for those
            who never sacrifice: (one very same thing

9:2-9:10   happens) to the good person as well as to the
hardened sinner, to the one who curses as well
as to the one afraid even to make a vow—
That is the wretched evil in all that is going on under
the sun, that the same blasted thing
hits everybody!
Granted that evil fills the heart of humans,
and insolence welters deep inside them
so long as they live, but—
finally, to the dead (you go). Yet, whoever is still
privileged to be among all the living has hope of sorts.

R1   "A live dog is better off than a dead lion"

Q   —because those still breathing are deeply conscious
that ... they have to die; while the dead are
conscious of absolutely nothing!
The dead get no recompense anymore,
not even the respect of being remembered.
Their love and hate and jealous passion is long
completely gone; not a lasting thing is allotted
them of all that is still going on under the sun.

(Look,)

Refr6   **Go eat your bread with gladness and drink your
wine with a merry heart whenever God has been
pleased so to bless your doings.
May your clothes sparkle bright at all times,
and may your head never have to do without
festive, perfuming oil.
Enjoy life with your beloved wife as long as you live
this fragile existence lent you under the sun:
(joy in your marriage) if that is allotted you
in your life and labour that you trouble yourself
so busily with in the world.
Whatever your hand finds to do, do it with all your
might! For there is no doings or "maneuverings"
either, no knowledge, no wisdom, there in the
grave where you are going.**

9:11-9:18

Q   So once more it became plain to me under the sun
           that the race goes not to the swift;
           the battle is not won by the strong-arm boys,
           and also, the wise do not necessarily get bread,
           nor persons with discernment amass riches,
           or those with insightful knowledge gain
           wide affection: changing times and what just
           happens strikes them all (despite their gifts).
       It also became plain to me that nobody ever
           recognizes when it is his or her turn—like fish
           caught in a frustrating net, or like birds trapped
           shut by an inviting cage, just so mortal humans
           stand there chagrined, stymied by the moment of
           calamity when it drops down without warning
           upon their heads.
       Another thing I saw around in the world, and it struck
           me as very significant for wisdom, was this:
       to a small city peopled with not so many
           inhabitants came a big-time king.
           He surrounded the city and lay siege with huge
           machines.
       Now there happened to be a poor man in that city
           who was wise, and he could have helped
           the city escape with his wisdom; but not a
           single person thought of asking that poor
           fellow (for help).
       So I put it this way: Wisdom may be favoured over
           heroics, but wisdom of an insignificant
           person is scorned, and none of what that
           person says is even heard.

R2   "Better than shouting of the most clever fool
       is what a wise man or woman says in quiet"
Q   —if heard!

R1   "Wisdom is better than weapons of war"
Q   but never forget, a single blunderer can ruin
       a mass of good!

10:1-10:10

R2   "A few dead flies decomposing can
     putrefy the oil stores of an ointment mixer";

Q   (just so) a little fickle stupidity (mixed in somewhere)
     carries more weight than wisdom and solid authority.

R1   "A wise person's sensitivity tends to be a (strong) right
     hand: but brains of a fool have a left-handed quirk."

Q   You can see it even on the street:
     when a fool takes a walk, his senses are missing, and
     everyone says to the other person, "That one there is
     a thick-headed, brainless fool."

R2   "If the ruler's anger starts to wind up over you,
      do not stop performing your task, for composure
      best leaves blustering wrongdoing nonplussed."

Q   That's an evil business I witnessed through
      the earth, how rash wrong committed
      by the potentate in command (ruined)—
      know-nothing insolence was set in honoured places
      by the score, while distinguished men and women
      were shunted off into some lowdown place.
     I saw sycophants riding high up on horses,
      while princely men
      walked the ground like slaves.

R1   "Who digs a hole in the ground could fall in it himself."
R2   "Who razes someone's wall,
      a (hidden) snake (in it) could bite."
R1   "Who smashes up stones could be bruised
      by them as well."
R2   "Who chops wood (with an ax) is endangered by the
     chippings."
R1   "If the iron ax-head becomes dull
      and one never sharpens its cutting edge,
      you have to exert all the more strength
      (to wield it)"
Q   —it would be worthwhile to do it right: wisdom.

10:11-11:1

R2   "If the snake bite before it is charmed,
                  what good is wizardry to the tongue spellbinder?"

R1   "Words spoken by a wise person work gentleness,
                  but the talk-talk-talk of a fool
                  grinds even himself to bits."

Q   The talk of foolish peoples' mouths
                  begins with frivolous chatter,
                  but ends in malicious impertinence.
                  The fool simply talks much too much—
                  a person just doesn't know what's going to happen,
                  and who could possibly tell you what shall take
                  place...in the wake of a fool!? The constant
                  busybodiedness of fools wears anybody out—
              why a fool doesn't even know
                  how to take a walk downtown!

R2   "Woe to you, O country, if your king be not of age
                  and the princely (regents) are still reveling at
                  the break of day."

R1   "Happy shall you be, O country,
                  if your king be noble bred, and your princes
                  eat at the right time for nourishment rather
                  than to get shamelessly drunk."

R2   "Indolent hands let the beams of a house
                  begin to sag, and if you are lazy enough,
                  the whole roof shall cave in."

R1   "People fix a meal for telling dirty jokes;
                  wine (they think) titillates living,
                  and money is an answer for everything."

Q   But do not wish the king ill even in your thoughts,
                  and don't you dare curse important people,
                  not even in the privacy of your bedroom:

R2   "A little heavenly bird might spirit the sound away;
                  some feathery thing just might spill the matter."

W   Go ahead, throw your bread freely out
                  upon the face of the water, because
                  after many, many days you shall find it back again.

11:2-11:9   That means:
                   give away to many and more
                   than many people whatever has been allotted
                   you, for you don't really know at all
                   what evil there is still to come
                   upon the earth:
               when the clouds get swollen with rain,
                   they disgorge it upon the ground, and
                   when a tree crashes to the earth southward,
                   or if it happens to be northward,
                   in the spot where the tree fell, there it lies.
               Still, whoever always watches the wind
                   (for fear it blow) never comes to sowing
                   (the seed), and habitual cloud-watchers
                   (for fear it rain) never gather in a harvest.
               Just as you are never able to know experientially
                   how the breath of life
                   like the little bones are formed
                   deep within the womb of a woman filled with child,
                   just so you shall never be able to come to know
                   through and through the doings of God,
                   the global mighty workings which God does.
               (Therefore), from crack of dawn to dusk,
                   sow your seed and do not let your hand be idle,
                   for you can never be knowing
                   what precisely will work, whether this
                   or that or both alike shall be worth doing.

Ref7   Yes, "Sweet is the light, and pleasant to the eyes
               it is to experience the warming sun."
           Yes, if a person lives many, many years,
               let him or her joy in them all:
               just let them not forget that the dark days,
               all those that come—an obscuring stinking mist—
               shall be many too.
           Enjoy yourself, fellow, while you are young!
               Let that red pulsing blood in you
               make you feel good that you are a young fellow.
           Do what you really feel like doing!
               Revel in whatever your eyes light upon

11:9-12:5 **—of course, know that in all these things,**
God will make you stand for judgment.
Get rid of things that disturb you deep down!
I hope you young fellows never get bodily sick,
because being young, having a flourishing beard ...
is an idle preoccupation soon past!

W   Remember the One who created you;
            think about that while you are a young fellow,
        before the evil days come, before the years creep up
            on you when you have to say,
            "That's not for me! I don't feel like it."
        (Keep an eye open for your Creator)
            before the sunlight stops, and the moon and stars
            turn dark, and dirty black clouds cover
            (everything again) and again after pouring rain.
        (Learn to recognize your Creator)
            before that Day when those who guard the house
            shall begin to tremble, and strong men
            will double themselves up (in fear);
        when women will stop working at the mill
            because too many have died,
            and those (left) looking out through the windows
            will fade away into the shadows;
        when doors open to the street will be shut
            at the eerie noise of the mill grinding down;
            when the (distant) chittering of birds
            will give you gooseflesh—all the little girls
            who used to sing will have been stilled;
        when people will even be scared to death
            of what's up in the air, and terrifying things
            will take place on the street—
        although the almond tree will be blossoming,
            the grasshopper will hardly be able to drag itself
            over the ground, and the salty caper berry
            will be tasteless.

12:5-12:12

Q   (Get close to your Creator before that Day)
              because then a man and a woman
              go to their eternal home, and those lamenting it
              will mill around in the street outside.

W   (Get close to your Creator)
              before the silver cord is taken away
              and the golden bowl is smashed to bits,
              before the pitcher near the spring of water
              is shattered and the waterwheel
              at the well is wrecked—

Q   the dust turns back to dirt as it once was,
              and the breath of life turns back to God
              who once gave it....

1st Voice   "Blasted nonsense—a fart!" the philosopher said.
              "It's all not worth a damn, a wild wind chase."
2nd Voice   But what about that Qohelet, a wise philosopher
              continually trying to teach the people knowledge
              (of good and evil)?
3rd Voice   ... And how about the fact that as philosopher-teacher,
              he spent time listening, testing, probing,
              fathoming (many) fascinating proverbs?
1st Voice   And what's written here is **right**!
2nd Voice   Reliable sayings that are **true**!
3rd Voice   (Yes), ... sayings of the (truly) wise are like sharp
              goads (used to nudge animals aright);
              the reflections gathered here,
              given by the one same Shepherd,
              are like tent pins firmly driven in ...
4th voice   Just one more thing, my good fellows,
(elderly)   you had better listen:
              there simply is no end to writing and reading;
              criticizing and working at books and books
              and books; and giving yourself to hem and haw
              investigation (on the meaning of everything)
              again and again and again is only wearing a body out.

12:13-12:14

(to aud.)   Do you know what all you have heard comes down to?

Chorus   **Stand in awe of God
and keep God's commandments!**

1st Voice   —That's something that's for everybody—

    All   Because every thing done
God will bring into just judgment,
all the things not found out too,
whether they were good or evil....

4
POST-PERFORMANCE COMMENTS

This approach of recognizing different voices emphasizes the unity of the book, and makes the translation of its complex literary character more literal, literarily literary.

You also heard what I call the "Yes, but" format of biblical wisdom literature. The LORD God's Older Testament prophets often spoke bluntly direct: Thus says the LORD, "Stop bringing me sacrifices! Instead, do what is just in society—protect the weak, defenseless ones!" (e.g., Isaiah 1:10-20). However, a godly wise woman from Tekoa made up and told a story to make indirectly known counsel for David to be reconciled with Absalom (II Samuel 14:1-20). Wise man, young King Solomon, said, "Cut the baby in half!" (I Kings 3:16-28). Yes, but not when the true mother speaks up. Rabbi Jesus told parables to get his point across to unreceptive audiences, for example, about: even Muslims are your neighbours (Luke 10:25-37).

So *Ecclesiastes* is not a mass of "contradictions"—that's what many commentators think—but follows the "Yes, but" format of "wisdom literature." The refrain interrupts and balances out Qohelet's battle with the Bombastic Stink of vicious killing Evil everywhere: "yes, it is so, but have you never tasted freshly baked bread with a glass of God's good red wine?" or "exulted in the joyful strength of good bodily sweat?" asks the refrain (2:24-26, 5:17-19).[1] The steady voice of Woman Wisdom offsets the unmistakable excruciating pain in Qohelet's lament (like Psalm 73), "How come the wicked flourish"?! "Yes, but do you realize that evil like sin is actually its own obliterating punishment" (8:2-8), says Woman Wisdom.

That is, important for understanding God's Word of *Ecclesiastes* is to recognize its unified wholeness and that the book exemplifies the "Yes, but" method of wise rabbis who make God's will known in this round-

---

1 Chaucer's wonderful line about the canon and his yeoman who had galloped on horses to catch up with their "joli compaignye" enroute to Canterbury embodies this sentiment of the 5:17-19 refrain: "But it was joye for to seen hym swete!" (*The Canterbury Tales, The Canon's yeoman's prologue*, VIII, 579).

about, literary allusive, parable-pedagogical way to give you as a disillu-
sioned Qohelet or as a bright young Pharisee lawyer debater the time to
tug and wiggle on God's line before the One Shepherd-Fisherman's hook
of love pulls you in to genuine wisdom.

Just a note about the historical setting of the book[2]

Ecclesiastes was probably booked c. 350 BC, when Persian King Ochus
Artaxerxes and his generals were fighting against the disintegration of their
worldly empire. Israel as a nation in the buffer military zone between Syria
and Egypt was in a mess. *Ecclesiastes* notes corruption at large in both the
legal system and the temple organization (3:16, 4:1, 5:7-8, 10:5,20). The
Jewish leadership at this time had such a defensive mentality they had set
up a theocracy in Jerusalem! So the climactic good news of Wisdom to
throw your bread freely out upon the surrounding waters (11:1-6) would
have sounded to God's people of that time like stark-raving madness. And
that's how the good news of *Ecclesiastes* sounds to any group of comfortable
Christians who may have their middle-class wagons drawn up in a defensive circle to protect their belongings: give away what you have?! (Mark
10:17-22, Matthew 19:16-22). Do it with your time and youthful energy
before the hard economic and fearful apocalyptic times come?! Why, the
voice of Wisdom in *Ecclesiastes* 11:1-12:7 sounds almost as crazy as what
Jesus Christ says in the Newer Testament: pray for those out to harm you!
(Matthew 5:38-48, Luke 6:27-31).

To grasp the meaning of *Ecclesiastes*, one needs to take in the narrative as one whole piece, and realize Qohelet, who thought he was struggling to make sense out of Evil and find something ever lasting, for a
while could not see that he was really challenging the everlasting Creator God who, like Wisdom beyond our ken (Job 28), reserves lasting,
rest-giving peace and shalom of blessing only for those who give up being
go-getters out to master the world, and give in to the call and gift of
Woman Wisdom—an alias for the Holy Spirit(!) in the Bible[3]—to trust

---

2. The fact that the name of "Solomon" is not mentioned anywhere in the book is a
    significant indication that the text was not booked by King Solomon, certainly not
    in his older age described by I Kings 9-11 (despite the vignette of how a king in Je-
    rusalem might mimic the parabola of Solomon's life). The term בני in 12:12 is strong
    evidence that the חכמים used by the LORD to write *Proverbs*, the *Greatest Song*, and
    Job were also used to book *Ecclesiastes*.
3. Cf. Exodus 31:1-5, Isaiah 11:1-5, Daniel 5:10-12. In a speech by Wisdom in Prov-
    erbs 1, verse 23 says, "I will pour out רוחי (my Spirit!) upon you." RSV and NRSV
    ("thoughts") and JB and NIV ("heart") have inadequate translations. KJ has it right.

(יְרֵא אֱלֹהִים)[4] that God's Way is merciful, even if it surprises and disturbs us self-centered human thinkers.

God gave God's Ten Words of guidance to Moses amid thunder and lightning to protect and liberate us, not to condemn us![5] God sent God's only son into the world as a Jew, to save us ethnics! (Galatians 3:23-29, Romans 9-11). God loves sinners and forgives them, rather than writes them off! (Ephesians 2:1-10). God gives God's children hard knocks, more so than the disbelievers whom the Bible calls illegitimate bastards (Proverbs 3:11-12, Hebrews 12:1-17). God spells out exorcizing curses for the covenanted faithful and followers of Christ to use, if they are themselves fasting and pure enough to utter them with forbearance.[6] God does pick up the broken pieces of our lives and the terrible sinful surds in history, believe it or not! (3:12-15).

Qohelet is somewhat like the scared Jacob at the brook Jabbok, who thought he was wrestling for his life with a strong man, but it turned out to be the angel of God (Genesis 32:22-32). Qohelet, who finally stops trying to "figure out" Evil rationally "and justify the ways of God to men,"[7] and who at last stops swallowing the sweet pop drinks of Woman Foolishness, finally hears Woman Wisdom's voice and accepts her embrace. Then Qohelet slowly—with a limp you could say—comes to trust and lament—the way the Psalms do—that God oversees the timing of events and taking care of good and evil (7:13-14), so we are freed up from cursing our lot, and instead, are primed for experiencing our daily troubled waking and sleeping hours as activity brimming over with Creator God's everlasting provident joys and justifying mercy, which last into the very apocalyptic end (Matthew 16:24-27, Hebrews 12:28-29).

Ecclesiastes, like the rest of the Bible, though it details the groaning of us creatures (Romans 8:18-39), is primarily about the great deeds of God. That's why one should grasp the final words of the book, not as a dogmatic command, but as a thankful cheer: **Stand in awe of God and keep God's commandments!**[8]

---

4. "Stand in awe of God" is spoken four times, first by Wisdom (5:6), then tentatively by Qohelet (7:18), then by Qohelet as a mark of the tried-and-true trusting doer of what is right (8:13), and finally by the responding chorus at the end of the book (12:13).
5. Cf. Exodus 19-20, Matthew 5:17-20, 6:19-7:27, John 3:17, Galatians 3.
6. Cf. Psalm 139:19-24, Matthew 17:14-21, Philippians 4:4-7.
7. John Milton, *Paradise Lost*, I,26.
8. *The Heidelberg Catechism* (1563) insightfully discusses the Ten Commandments, not in its section on "Sin," but in its third section under the rubric of "Gratitude."

5

ACTUAL PERFORMANCE
HISTORY OF *ECCLESIASTES*

Pre-history

The graduate Institute for Christian Studies appointed me to the chair of philosophical Aesthetics in September 1972. At that time the Senior Members (the name used for "professors," to distinguish them from the graduate "students," who were called Junior members) were asked to go on speaking tours throughout Canada and the USA, to centers of supporters of the Institute, to hint at what we were teaching. In January 1973 I took my completed translation of *Ecclesiastes* on the road to several cities (Chicago, Grand Rapids, Edmonton, Vancouver and St. Catharines as well as Toronto).

For each setting I sent ahead of time the following sheets of instructions to a "co-ordinator," who would prospect for the competent voices and the musicians needed to play the interludes (I forwarded some of the appropriate sheet music too). Professor John Worst was the musician in Grand Rapids at the old Calvin Seminary; Lynnell Fennema played the musical fragments in Chicago; and Bert Polman did the music in Toronto, including the final doxology. I do not remember who the local musicians were in the other cities.

On the scheduled evening I would give a brief lecture on what was happening and why, and then read my translation of the whole book of *Ecclesiastes* with the chorus of assigned voices. And then there was time for a Q&A with the audience.

To co-ordinator of choral readers and musical interludes for the reading of *Ecclesiastes*: the following voices are needed to read the designated script at the appropriate places:

Announcer-type male voice	Contralto woman voice
Good, clear speaking male voice	Soprano woman voice
Statesmanlike voice	Saucy woman voice
Loud self-satisfied voice	Matter-of-fact male voice

Voices for the conclusion

Excited young teenage boy voice	Elderly person with still strong
Late 20-year old woman voice	commanding voice that the
30-year old woman voice	assembled people will respect

When the lecture is given, the voices should be seated on the periphery of the audience. I should like to work out with the voices an hour before the program begins. I hope they shall have the lines almost memorized so they can be spoken easily and authoritatively.

Music serves as commentator interlude on what is coming in the text of *Ecclesiastes.*

Piano: *Chopsticks* … schmalzy *Danny Boy* … snatch of Mozart … dissonant (modern) music snatch … back to *Chopsticks* unfinished: **1:2-2:26**

About a page and a half of Beethoven's *Moonlight sonata:* **3:1-15**

My country 'tis of Thee/God save the Queen played through in a minor key: **3:16-4:16**

Last phrase of minored *My country, 'tis of Thee* moving into chorus of Elgar's *Land of Hope and Glory* (or in Canada, *Ere zij God*): **4:17-5:6**

Last phase again of minored *My Country, 'tis of Thee:* **5:7-6:9**

Single tone line of Gregorian chant for a bit, moving into some counterpoint Bach: **6:10-7:24**

Guitar: Leonard Cohen, *Suzanne*, one or maybe two stanzas, to be sung: **7:25- 8:15**

Piano again: Welsh hymn *Alleluia! Alleluia!* (Psalter Hymnal #360):
8:16-9:12

Brass quartet responsive echoing section well known in Brahm's
Variations on a theme of Haydn symphony (or something
suggesting a richer playback type of counterpoint than the
baroque- line of Bach above)—on piano: **9:13-10:20**

Guitar again: *Michael row the boat ashore* (first verse two times):
11:1-12:14

Piano & guitar with assembly singing doxology from: Psalm 72
(Psalter Hymnal #488)

History

(1) 2010 Spain

Initial performance on 30 October 2010, San Lorenzo de El Escoriel,
Spain as part of the program of the 11th Spanish Arts Gathering and a
joint event with the XXVII National Intervarsity Conference for Gradu-
ates. Castillian Spanish version translated by Marga Llavador, directed by
Amalia F. Romero, produced by Joyce Phillips.

Qohelet	James Phillip
Woman Wisdom	Amalia F. Romero
Editor	Llorenç Torras
Apprentice Rabbi A	Julie Barshinger
Apprentice Rabbi B	Antonio Soto
Refrain Trio of Voices	Sara Tutusaus, Ana Rando
	Nicolás Couvreux
Musical interludes	Marcos Cob
Artworks background	Antonio Soto
Voice 4	Prof. David Estrada

San Lorenza, de El Escorial, Spain.

Speaker Seerveld and Spanish translator of *Ecclesiastes*,
Marga Llavador, October 2010

The Castilian Spanish translation, *Palabras de Cohelet, hijo de David, rev de Jerusalem*, can be available upon request from Joyce Phillips at info@ artsgathering.info.

(2) 2011 USA

30 September 2011, Cornerstone University, Grand Rapids, Michigan USA, directed by Randall Burghart, produced by Matthew Bonzo.

Qohelet	Matthew Elmore
Woman Wisdom	Carolyn Quinn-Allen
Editor	Steven Haskill
Apprentice rabbi A	Rachel Anderson
Apprentice rabbi B	Ian Grell

Refrain Dancers: Sarah Grace (McDaniel) Groot and two others

Extensive musical interludes by a Kurt Weill Brechtian band:

Thomas Mossv	piano
Joan Van Dessell	clarinet
Michael Stockdale	guitar
Eric Scholtens	electric bass

With a cameo piano performance by Michael Card who happened to be present at Cornerstone University for a gig.

Musical interludes (discretely performed live rather than recorded) were suggested as allusive commentaries on the spoken word, to either encapsulate what was said or prepare for what will be spoken, and to give listeners a selah moment to digest audibly what they are hearing. The suggestions here made were carefully and mostly followed by director Burghart, although they were tentative at the time, and should naturally be modified to fit the performance environs, e.g. a Basque folk tune or a Spanish national anthem should replace the North American suggestions, and instrumentation available, e.g. cello rather than piano.

1. Potpourri of Piano *Chopstick*s, schmalzy *Danny Boy*, snatch of Mozart, then dissonant modern music snatch, back to *Chopsticks* unfinished.
   1:2-11 Problem: what's left of all of a man or woman's work on earth?

2. Beethoven's *Moonlight Sonata*, a couple of pages of first movement on piano.

1:12-2:16 Search as ostensible potentate for the meaning of being alive under the sun.

3. Chorus of Elgar's *Land of Hope and Glory* ending in dissonant chords.
    2:17-2:23 & 2:24-26 (Refrain I) Disappointment ending in a question.

4. Back to *Moonlight Sonata* continued into last movement a bit, modulating into a Bach oratorio, beginning only.
    3:1-15 *God picks up the pieces* [WISDOM] incl. 3:12-3:15 (Refrain II).

5. Closing chorale of Bach's *St Matthew Passion on "rest."*
    3:16-21,22 Observations of evil, and humans die, like animals (echo refrain II).

6. Sung phrases of *Dies Irae* moving into Genevan 51 psalm melody halfway.
    4:1-4:16 On the violated, better dead, lonely singles, young rather than old king.

7. Snatch of Elgar's chorus + *God Save the Queen/My Country 'tis of Thee* in minor key and moving into opening plainchant of the Easter mass.
    4:17-5:6 [English 5:1-5:7] Going to worship is dangerous if you talk a lot [WISDOM voice].

8. African American spiritual *Steal away* + fragment of *God Save the Queen* in minor key.
    5:7-5:16 & 5:17-5:19 (refrain III) [Eng 5:8-20]
    On corrupt government, business failure, but God can give joy.

9. *Joy to the World* hymn but back to *Danny Boy* melody and *Chopsticks*.
    6:1-6:12 It is best to be stillborn! No guaranteed consequences ever.

10. Selection from Mahler's *Kindertoten Lieder* moving into a counter point exercise.

7:1-7:12 & 7:13-14 Exercise in "Better-than" "wisdom" debate (crucial refrain IV).

11. *Under the double Eagle* jazz piece, moving into Bach chorale ending. **7:15-7:24** Proverbial "wisdom" cannot fathom God's deep mystery of deeds among us.

12. Muddy Waters Blues piece and then Cohen's *Suzanne* song, a couple of phrases. **7:25-29** Seduction is real, and seeker could not find Woman Wisdom.

13. Welsh hymn Ton-y-botl. 8:9-8:14 & 8:15 (refrain V) Psalm 73 talk: the wicked prosper/the good suffer, yet receive joy if it be given to you.

14. Blues on into Brahm's brass quartet on *Variations* on Haydn symphony. **8:16-9:6 & 9:7-10** (refrain VI) + 9:11-9:12 Humans cannot penetrate God's mysterious care of creatures, so accept the gift of health, food, bodily love.

15. Snatch of the Brahms modulating to *Michael, Row the Boat Ashore*. **9:13-10:20** A single fool can actually upset wisdom, and Power can be utterly foolish.

16. Counterpoint Bach + Minor key piece of *God Save the Queen* moving into fearsome movie theme song & then selection from Haydn's bright, hopeful *Creation* oratorio. **11:1-11:6** Give away your gifts, which God provides [WISDOM voice].

17. Vigorous jazz piece. **11:7-11:10** Enjoy whatever God allots to your life (refrain VII).

18. 1686 Dancing Master tune to *All things Bright and Beautiful* hymn **12:1-12:7** Remember your Creator before the apocalypse comes [WISDOM voice].

19. Selection from Bach's *St Matthew passion* and Mahalia Jackson's *Moving on up a Little Higher*. **12:8-12:14** Resolved: stand in awe before God and do God's will.

20. Genevan 89 psalm tune, with those present singing the *Paean of Joy* (Seerveld text, stanza 1).

> How shall we thank you, Lord, for joy and this surprise?
> You have come through again to recreate our lives.
> We stand amazed: Your providential hand
> looks after our struggling daily cares;
> Your kiss fills mouths with laughter.
> Hear our excited shouts, Lord, spirits now are buoyant.
> Your simple miracle turns trouble into triumph.

[This melody of Genevan 89 is probably not possible since the tune is not well known to a USA audience. Maybe all could sing *Praise God from whom all blessings flow* à tempo (with words on program for strangers, but not print the well-known tune). Or one just ends without audience participating in the psalm/hymn song (?)]

(3) 2011 USA

6, 8 and 9 October 2011, Trinity Christian College, Palos Heights, and downtown Grace Chicago Church, Illinois USA, directed by Dr. John S. Sebestyen, voiced by Trinity faculty, alumni, and students, sponsored by the Departments of Communication Arts, Philosophy, Sociology, and Theology at Trinity Christian College, produced by Dr. Brad Breems.

Qohelet	Dr. Craig Mattson
Woman Wisdom	Camille Villegas
Editor	Dr. Dave Larsen
Apprentice rabbi A	Jacob Szafranski
Apprentice rabbi B	Aaron Visser
Refrain	Dr. Aron Reppmann, Jane Voss, Teryn Leaper
Responding voices	Trinity Faculty Members,
Lighting designer	Bridget Earnshaw
Live musical interludes	James Falzone, Bells, gongs, recorders and the launeddas (Sardinian instrument used in the shepherdic folk traditions), freshly composed.

(4) 2011 Canada

For a full week of afternoons and evenings Redeemer University College theatre department performed, for a paying audience in Southern Ontario, both *The Greatest Song* and *Ecclesiastes,* translated by Seerveld as choruses of voices.

Only the *Ecclesiastes* event is listed here. Director Carson decided the Qohelet character was too much for one student voice to carry; so he ingeniously assigned the text split to two different voices. Graphic images of Qohelet's experiences were portrayed as a dumb show on sheets surrounding the in-person performers, which was visible to the audience seated on the stage.

22-26 November 2011, Redeemer University College, Ancaster, Ontario Canada, student performance directed by Tom Carson. Sponsored by the Redeemer University College Theatre Arts Department, produced by Sharon Klassen.

Qohelet	Kaitlyn McGee, Nathan Hicks
Woman Wisdom	Paige Louter
Editor	Jonathan Silverhorn
Apprentice rabbi A	Jessica Watson
Apprentice rabbi B	Meghan Colquhoun
Refrain	Catherine Hordyk
Stage manager	Kaitlin Vandersluis
Musical Director	Jeanine Noyes (music originally composed and taped)

(5) 2014 Canada

12 March 2014, Tyndale University College and Seminary, Toronto, Ontario Canada, directed by Tom Carson, sponsored by The Arts Engine Company

Qohelet	Raymond Louter
Woman Wisdom	Clarissa Der Nederlanden-Taylor
Editor	Calvin Seerveld
Apprentice rabbi A and B	Local persons
Refrain	Clarissa Der Nederlanden-Taylor
Musical interludes	Wendy Solomon (cello)

Since this cast assembled by director Tom Carson had reached a high level of professional competence, it was decided to take the performance of *Ecclesiastes* to the general populace, both to honour the dedicated work of the voicing speakers and to make this enigmatic Bible book better known.

(6) 6 April 2014, Meadowland Christian Reformed Church (Sunday evening), Ancaster, Ontario, Canada.

(7) 12 April 2014, Rehoboth Fellowship Christian Reformed Church (Saturday evening), Toronto, Ontario, Canada.

(8) 13 April 2014, Willowdale Christian Reformed Church (Sunday evening), Toronto, Ontario, Canada.

(9) 17 April 2014, Crossfire Assembly (Thursday evening), Hamiton, Ontario, Canada.

(10) 18 September 2014, Unauthorized in-house production at Redeemer University, Ancaster, Ontario, Canada.

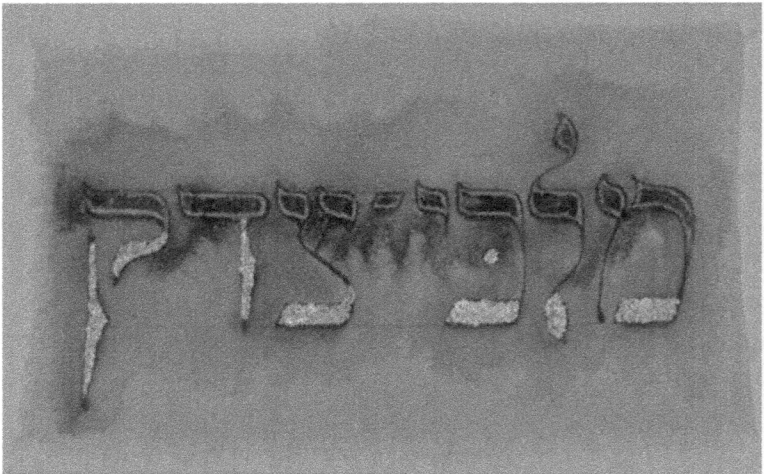

Melchizedek. 2019, coloured blue ink and gold on cloth, Michael Carter

The mysterious Melchizedek, a priest-king of just-doing and peace
(Genesis 14:17-20, Hebrews 7:1-3), is certified by Psalm 110:4 as the
Christian believers' calling to lead by serving, and to
rule by washing your neighbour's feet.

6

EXEMPLARY CRITICAL RESPONSES

An honest critical question from one of God's believing people

From: T.A.
Date: April 7, 2014
Subject: *Ecclesiastes*

I was at Meadowlands CRC last night and saw a production of *Ecclesiastes*. I must say that I was impressed by the amount of memorization that the two main actors did for the performance, and I appreciated that much of what was said was true to the Biblical text. However, I was shocked by some of the language that was used. I certainly did not expect what was advertised in my church bulletin as "a Lenten evening of worship" to include bad language. There is just something very wrong with adding profanity to a Biblical text when we are told repeatedly in the Bible NOT to curse, use profanity, or let any unwholesome talk come out of our mouths. I don't know if it was added so that the reading would appear edgy and cool, or if it was added for shock value. It is most unfortunate since this really put a blight on an excellent presentation. Perhaps you could share my concern with Dr. Seerveld since I do not have contact information for him; he may wish to reconsider and edit his text. As a side note, two other people who were at the play approached me and expressed the same concern, so I'm sure there are others. Thank-you for your time,

T.A.

From: Tom Carson
To: Cal Seerveld
Monday, April 07, 2014 10:06 PM
Subject: Fwd: *Ecclesiastes*

Hi Cal,

Thought you might like to reply to this. I would love to be cc'd on your response.

Take care,
Tom Carson

From: Calvin Seerveld
To: T.A.
Sent: Tuesday, April 08, 2014

Dear T.A.,
Thank you for your response to Tom. I appreciate your concern, and for raising the question about the language of "damned" and "fart" in the presentation of the biblical book of *Ecclesiastes*. Your concern is why I prefer to give an introduction before the performance, to take away the shock of the strong language. In my judgment there should at least be a Q & A discussion session over coffee after such a performance. The oral reading of the Bible is not a theatre piece, as I see it, but an attempt to get believers and unbelievers present to hear the passionate God speaking to our human needs, to convict us of our sin and lead us to be repentant. I believe the Bible is God-speaking literature. But many do not take the literary character of the Bible seriously.

When Lady Macbeth in Shakespeare (*Macbeth* V, 1) is trying to wipe off King Duncan's blood from her little murderous hands, and says, "Out! Damned spot—out, I say!" she is not loosely cursing, but agonizes at the crux of a very moral theatre piece in realizing the irretrievable damning guilty evil of her deed.

When the prophet Ezekiel, son of a priest called to be spotlessly pure, immaculate, when serving the perfect Holy God with unblemished sacrifices, describes the cheap offerings of God's people and their humdrum adulteries, Ezekiel develops an extremely colourful, scatological vocabulary for "whoring" and "sin" to give vent to the outrage of God, who made us men and women innocent creatures without guile, and look what puny, preening filthy hypocrites we have become! For example, read out loud Ezekiel 23:17-21. That's in the Bible! But you don't hear many sermons on the ads in our magazines and what such incitement does to us who read them.

That is, while the strong language may make you feel uncomfortable as being in the Bible, I think it presents the biblical Hebrew God-breathed text accurately. The Qohelet character in *Ecclesiastes* has doggedly spent a philosophical lifetime searching existentially for the meaning of things, and is utterly frustrated. Not only "wine-women-and-song" (1:12-2:11), but riches, recognition, solid hard-earned achievements (2:12-23)—all these shimmering bubbles have always burst! We men and women die like animals (3:18-21); the healthy-wealthy-and-wise stop breathing as well as those unfortunates mired in poverty, or the stupids of the world (5:12-16). What a waste! It's a crime, a damn shame! Death is wrong! It is a curse! Everything is really meaningless!, ... isn't it? We need to hear this fellow struggling to make sense of God's world full of injustices, hurts, atrocities. It's a damned life, isn't it? (I know, most people who have a fairly comfortable life would rather say more politely, "Yes, it's a cursed life out there ... in Rwanda, isn't it?")

The "dramatic" point of the whole *Ecclesiastes* book is how the Woman Wisdom voice (an Older Testament presentation of the Holy Spirit, I think—which there was no opportunity for me to tell to those present) changes Qohelet from a cursing disgruntled fellow who looks evil creaturely reality right in the eye, into one who gradually comes to say in his heart and reluctant voice, "It is so, I took everything to heart, and this much I got clear, that the tried-and-true folk and the wise and all their on-going deeds rest in the hand of God" (9:1, after 7-8 of the 12 chapters). Did you notice how Qohelet's language changes after chapter 7?

Much more could be said. Too many believers, it seems to me, want to avoid the rough side of the Bible. Psalm 139:19 says, "O that you would kill the wicked, O God!" (NRSV). Should we omit that sentence from God's Word since we are told by Jesus to love our enemies? I do not think so. But we need to read it aloud in the literary whole of the Psalm, and realize the Psalm quickly says, "Search me, O God, and know my heart" (v.23) lest I be found to be wicked and You need to kill me!" (The new *Lift Up your Hearts* song book for the church leaves out the curse in Psalm 139; cf. #336, #337).

Maybe I dare say, a minister came up to me afterwards and said privately, "This would not go in my congregation." I am sorry about that, since I think then that congregation misses a terrific message of good news from the Bible. God came to save dirty, cursing sinners like Qohelet, sinners, the apostle Paul says, "of whom I am chief" (KJ, I Timothy 1:15).

Hoping this gives you an idea of how our conversation could go, and thanking you for taking the time to write T, I am sincerely yours,

Calvin Seerveld

Probing question from a trusted colleague

Nelvin L. Vos is a professor of English literature and a drama specialist, at Lutheran Muhlenberg College, Allentown, Pennsylvania USA, to whom I sent the translation of Ecclesiastes manuscript.

From: Nelvin L. Vos
Date: July 25-14
To: Calvin Seerveld
Subject: *Ecclesiastes*

Hello, Cal,
Well, as usual, your translations are very lively and provocative. And I suspect, some would say "loose" or an even more condemnatory word.

For example, 7:3—what you propose seems a long way from and less direct than "Sorrow is better than laughter."

Or, I was not aware that vanity and fart were in the same neighborhood of meaning. 2:17 includes "what the hell"? It's not that I necessarily object to this language but how do you determine the power of the original?

And in the same vein, the attribution of speech to individuals is not always clear to me. I guess what I'm asking you is this: What is the rationale or justification for this creative enterprise?

In brief, I admire and respect your very hard work on this but I am wondering about its intent and purpose.

By the way, I would give a medal to the person who tracked down all the music you suggested! (for the Cornerstone University performance, see above pp. 55-58).

Nelvin

From: Calvin Seerveld
Date: November-04-14
Subject: Re: *Ecclesiastes*

Dear Nelvin,
Let me try to respond to your good questions about *Ecclesiastes*.

Qohelet 7:3: I would maintain that the Hebrew text is more quirky than "Sorrow and laughter." The best Hebrew dictionary (Koehler-Baumgartner —I studied Hebrew with Baumgartner in Basel, 1955, one of the last living "Higher Critics") gives for *k'am* the translation "*Unmut kraenkung,* vexation, grief," and for *sechoq* "clumsy playing around for the amusement of others." As an authority on "laughter," you know the many possible varieties! Buber, whom I always check, has for 7:3a: "*Besser ist Verdrossenheit als Gelaechter.*" "*Verdrossen*" has the connotations of being sulky, sullen, annoyed; and "*Gelaechter*" has overtones of being a laughing-stock for others.

So a good translation, in my judgment, is not always the more 'direct' and generic equivalent; try to gather up the nuances in the new language.

'Vanity' comes from the sloughing off that happened with the vulgate translation of *hebel* as *vanitas* in Latin. The Septuagint *maiotes* ('emptiness') had already lost the metaphoric image of *hebel* which means 'noxious hot air' (Buber: *Dunst*, fumes). *Hebel* also has the side meaning of being pretentious and meaningless; *hebel* is used by the prophets to refer to idols. So current readers are short-changed if they think `vanity' is someone primping before a mirror. Vanity, according to the Bible, is much worse than many people today think; vanity is being obnoxious, fake, dirty. (Fox and others translate it 'absurd,' after Camus! But that is too intellectual a choice, I think.)

That is why 2:17, which sums up 2:12-16, sounds out the narrator's exasperation: (NRSV) `So I hated life, because what is done under the sun was grievous to me; for all is vanity and a chasing after wind.' Because both 'vanity' and 'chasing wind' (N.B. 'passing gas'!) occur together here, the speaker is expostulating to the extent of swearing about the utter 'fruitless, meaningless stink to all existence—'What the hell.'

The attribution of text to individual is a deeper, intuited (but defensible) matter. Gordis has demonstrated, I think, the practice of 'quotation' is natural to 'wisdom literature' in the Bible. And a chorus of voices is a sound feature of such writing too (cf. Job, *The Greatest Song,* my article on *Proverbs*, chapter 10:1-22 in Stek Festschrift). I think I make sense of chapters 7 and 10 in *Ecclesiastes* by showing that Qohelet, as 'master rabbi,' corrects or modifies or confirms other & earlier 'proverbs,' voiced by others. Determining which sentences are earlier quotations and which are minted by Qohelet for the occasion is moot, but has the coherence once one determines the searching character of Qohelet. My 'find' of the Woman Wisdom voice would take longer to explain, since it ties *Ecclesiastes* to *Proverbs* chapter 9 and corrects what many wrongly take as a misogynistic remark in *Ecclesiastes* 8:28.

I intend to give voice to the chorus of voices, which the biblical *Ecclesiastes* text presents. The Bible must become oral, to be heard. And as God's Word it needs to be heard in its lively, confronting, intimate appeal, both serious and playful, complex and simple. Our Bibles must not be domesticated, but faced in God's vocative intensity.

The performance at Cornerstone University College in Grand Rapids did indeed track down the musical suggestions! A kind of Brecht-Weill ragtag band with a great pianist, clarinetist (for the Gershwin rhapsody wail), acoustic bass, and a special brief cameo performance by Michael Card (who happened to be at the college). At Trinity a single percussive jazz musician used gongs and recorder and pipes to initiate the various segments. In Ontario we have been using a superb cellist who works with most of the suggestions.

Much more could be said, but I can't get back to *Ecclesiastes* until late winter.

Cal

7
NOTES FOR PRODUCING PERFORMANCES

Conception

Crucial to understanding the biblical book of *Ecclesiastes* is recognizing that there are several voices addressing the common unifying topic of "What does everything mean? Is hope available to humans in this troubled historical world of God?"

But the different voices in the text are not so clearly delineated as they are in the book of *Job* (God, Satan, Job, Job's wife, Eliphaz, Bildad, Zophar, Elihu). However, it is clear that the narrative of *Ecclesiastes* is set up as if someone is reporting what a character called "Qohelet" says (title 1:1, 7:27, 12:8-9,). We could call this reporting author-person "Editor." Given the "Yes, but" fabric to biblical "wisdom literature," one might expect a countering positive refrain to the excruciating, sad monologue of the "I saw evil," "I experienced violence" narrator. And there is a sevenfold, very joyful affirmation of possible happy world events sprinkled through the whole piece, as well as an obvious coda (12:8-14) commenting upon what has happened, which closes the book. Following my treatment of the collected book of *Proverbs*, it makes sense to grapple with the profusion of quotable epigrams, especially in chapters 7 and 10 of *Ecclesiastes*, as a kind of challenging sport of novice rabbis on who has the most appropriate proverbs to fit the topic. (These are the kind of competitions, I imagine, wisemen held in the ancient East circles, at which Solomon was a champion; see I Kings 4:29-34).

Also, one can clarify the oppositional tension at play in the book of *Ecclesiastes* by designating certain far-reaching, deep-going passages of the back-and-forth "Yes, but" temper to a Woman Wisdom character, who is so predominant in the book of *Proverbs* (1:20-33, 8:1-36, 9:1-6) and very clarifying to a climactic turning point in the book of *Ecclesiastes* at 7:23-29.

Possible characters of the voices

Editor (1) A prologue editor voice (a fairly gruff laborer in working over-alls) 1:2-11, 7:27, & 8:1.

Qohelet (2) Qohelet (main speaker, articulate sensitive mature baritone/bass man voice, 35-50 year old academic) means "an encyclopedic gatherer and leader." Luther translated the term as "Preacher," and most current English translations make it "Teacher."

Woman wisdom (3) WISDOM (contralto woman rich voice, mature matron 50-70 years old, deliberate and poetic speaker, as if it be the believing conscience or guardian angel of Qohelet is preferably a woman of color who speaks key passages of the book) 3:1-15,22 & 4:17-5:6 [Eng 5:1-7], 8:2-8, 11:1-6, 12:1-7.

Refrain (4) Sevenfold refrain [**bold text**] (to be spoken in chorus by 3 dancers—as one voice or a sequence of voices—with choreographed movement) 2:24-26, 3:12-15, 22 (spoken by Wisdom but danced by chorus), 5:17-19 [Eng 5:18-20], 7:13-14, 8:15, 9:7-10. 11:7-10.

(5) Two dueling proverb quoters, A & B (good, quick, polished voices, could be a man and a woman—young rabbis in training, so to speak—delivered as if to say, "Can you top this?" as relevant commentary. Qoheleth often follows up to give a concluding still wiser saying.)

R1 proverb quoter A: 1.15a, 2.14a, 4.9, 5.2[3], 5.9a[10a], 5.10a[11], 7.1a, 7.3a, 7.5, 7.8b, 7.19, 8.5a, 9.4b, 9.18a, 10.2, 10.8a, 10.9a, 10.10ab, 10.12, 10.17, 10.19.

R2 proverb quoter B: 1.18a, 4.5a, 4.12c, 5.4, 5.6[7], 5.9b[10b], 7.1b, 7.3b, 7.6, 7.8a, 7.21, 9.1b, 9.17ab, 10.1a, 10.4, 10.8b, 10.9b, 10.11, 10.16, 10.18, 10.20bc.

(6) **Closing voices of Response** (could be situated, miked, in the congregated audience, moving toward the front as they rise to speak): 1st, quite young teenager voice; 2nd, late 20-year-old-woman voice; 3rd, 30-year-old-woman voice; 4th, elderly strong-commanding-man voice the audience will respect.

Paragraphs (a possible fairly cohesive sectioning of the *Ecclesiastes* text) to help determine shifts in the conversation and to suggest selahs for musical interludes.

The book *Ecclesiastes* is a chorus of voices biblically exploring a response to the problem: Is there really any sense to all the efforts we humans exert on the earth? These various voices explore the life-problem in the biblical wisdom (rabbi, back-and-forth) way.

1:2-11 PROLOGUE: Author-editor sums up Qohelet's endeavour, to find out what's left over from all of a man or woman's (עמל) grueling hard labour) on earth.

1:12-2:11,12-16 Qohelet's search as potentate for the meaning of being alive under the sun

2:17-23, Incessant work (עמל) yields (הבל)
 2:24-26 (refrain I) simple gifts?

3:1-15 WISDOM voice: Apparent mindless routine? No, God's timing is just (inklings for us).
 3:12-15 (refrain II) God picks up the pieces!

3:16-21 Qohelet's observations of evil: He sees that humans die, like animals.
 3:22 (echo refrain II)

4:1-4:16 Qohelet on oppressions: Self-defeating aggression, existing alone, need companion

4:17-5:6 WISDOM voice [English 5:1-5:7]: In God's house be circumspect, especially regarding vows, chatter.

5:7-5:16 [Eng 5:8-20] Qohelet on corrupting government & business; reverses bring misery.
 5:17-5:19 (refrain III) But God can give joy in human (עמל) hard labour

6:1-6:9 Best to be stillborn! Consequences of עמל never assured.

6:10-12 Human mortals cannot dispute with God on **what is good**.

7:1-12 Proverbial "Better-than" "wisdom" is limited, only relatively worthwhile.
7:13-14 (refrain IV) Be amazed at God's doings—in charge of bad as well as good days!

7:15-7:22 Show-off righteousness is fake? Awe of God saves you from both.

7:23-29 Qohelet: by persistent investigation into human connivance I found ... (את־האשה) **the Woman (Folly)—v27** Author-editor comments—Qohelet: I found one good (אדם) person, but never found (ואשה) **Woman (Wisdom)**.
Therefore, (מצאתי) I "figured out" God made humans good, but humans devise strategies.

8:1 Author-editor: what would a wise person be like?

8:2-8 WISDOM voice: Obey God's ruler; humans are not in control; know Evil takes its toll.

8:9-14 Chastened Qohelet: live in awe of God, but wicked flourish Psalm 73 means ... הבל.
8:15 (refrain V) Receive joy if God gives it to you.

8:16-9:6 Beyond-figuring-out-God-aware Qohelet affirms (הצדיקים) tried-and-true folk and (החכמים) the wise rest in God's hand, so despite wretched death, live!
9:7-10 (refrain VI) Enjoy married life and act vigorously before death comes.

9:11-9:12 Wising-up Qohelet admits effort is not insurance against sudden calamity.

9:13-10:20 A single fool can ruin wisdom; wise proverbial sayings abound, but beware....

11:1-11:6 WISDOM voice: Do not delay; freely give away your gifts which God provides.

11:7-11:10 (refrain VII) Enjoy whatever God allots your life, aware of judgment coming.

12:1-12:7 WISDOM voice (Qohelet 12:5c slipped in):
Remember your Creator **before** the apocalypse comes.

12:8-12:14 EPILOGUE: Respondents clammer that Qoheleth was a searching wise man who thought everything was הבל; so the point of it all is to stand in obedient awe of God and do God's will, because God's (במשפט) just judgment on good and evil is certain.

Possible text for a printed Program with El Don painting by Antonio Soto on the cover.

The canonic book of *Ecclesiastes* in the Bible, like the book of *Job*, employs several different voices to bring us God's good news.

The main speaker in *Ecclesiastes*, Qohelet, is trying to find out what all our hard work and troubles mean. Is human effort just a lot of foul hot air? As the book of James puts it, "Are we just a mist that appears for a little while and then vanishes?" (James 4:14)

There is a voice of Woman Wisdom in *Ecclesiastes*, which gradually convinces Qohelet that God picks up the pieces of our lives, and that to stand in awe of God is the beginning of true wisdom (as it says in Proverbs 1:7, 9:10). In fact, the Woman Wisdom voice in *Ecclesiastes* resounds like the Lady Wisdom, who speaks in Proverbs, chapters 1 and 8.

There is also a sevenfold refrain in *Ecclesiastes,* which offsets Qohelet's frustrated search, and helps make the positive point of the book: joy in God's good creation under God's sun when the LORD gives you the opportunity.

The fisherman apostle Peter said some of educated apostle Paul's letters are difficult to understand (II Peter 3:14-16). When a person realizes the Holy Spirit uses a unified circle of voices in the book of *Ecclesiastes* to tell us humans what it takes to be wise, then this vivid book of the Bible becomes very intelligible, deeply relevant for our time and place, and able to convict us humans at heart to hear and obey and to cheer God's Word.

Concluding comment

The copyrighted nature of this multiple voice translation of *Ecclesiastes* is not meant to discourage people from attempting its production, but to promote (if possible) the spirit in which it can be done, either in a Spanish palace or in your local church or community building. Can we reform the Humanistic performance practice of "We artists will not context for you what we are doing"?

Whether the *Ecclesiastes* piece is "proclamation" and/or "theatre" and deserves an introduction, is moot. However, even if brief comment at the beginning be inappropriate, a post-performance Q & A with the Voices would be desirable.

Sometimes I offered the following prayer in certain settings before the recitation of *Ecclesiastes* began:

Dear God,
Please let your Holy Spirit fill this place
so that those who speak and play music, and listen intently,
shall be able to give voice to, and to hear, how much You love us
      in our often mixed-up lives.
Thank you, Lord, for the biblical book of *Ecclesiastes* in all its
      complexity, which gets to the heart of us mortals,
whose hopes are often staggered by disappointments and suffering.
Give us the peace now and the openness to be touched deeply for good
      by your rough, redemptive Word.
We pray You hear us, in the Name of Jesus Christ, Amen.

This prayer, even if unspoken, articulates well the spirit in which the performance of "God picks up the pieces" can best be spoken in public.

8

ARTWORKS REINFORCING INSIGHTS OF *ECCLESIASTES*

Different artists in different ages, including today, have struggled, like Qohelet, to understand what Pascal called *la gloire et le misère de l'homme*. Women and men can enjoy simple pleasures, but commit and suffer terrible evil, and we are mortal. Does it all somehow have meaning? Can the oppressed and disconsolate be comforted in God's world by wisdom or love?

Vase of flowers in a window, by Ambrosius Bosschaert the Elder (1573-1621)

Still life with gilt goblet (1635), Willem Claesz. Heda, 1593/1594-c. 1680/1682, Museum Boijmans van Benningen, Rotterdam

Small Dutch oil paintings of the 1600s AD often show wondrous bouquets of exotic flowers like tulips mixed in with ordinary irises and roses, to showcase the stunning loveliness of such colourful creatures. But in Qohelet fashion, near the vase would often be a fallen bloom or a fly which lives only a few days, a *memento mori*, in the event you were forgetting we humans are also perishable goods like cut flowers, soon thrown out and forgotten (cf. *Ecclesiastes* 2:12-16). An exquisitely painted still life on wood panel exults in the texture of pewter, the glory of a lovely glass holding liquid, the tempting luscious look and smell of fresh oysters on the half shell. But you notice a dish is knocked over, one glass is bro-

Man with a hoe, Jean François Millet
(1814-1897). J. Paul Getty Museum.

Black woman scrubbing a floor (1967),
Jacob Lawrence

This is Harlem, Jacob Lawrence, (1943).

Tombstones,
Jacob Lawrence, (1972).

ken in pieces, and the peeled lemon is drying out, as if someone had to leave abruptly and didn't come back. Yes, appreciate the gift of good food and drink before it be disrupted by death (*Ecclesiastes* 12:6-7), which is always an interruptive shock (cf. I Thessalonians 5:1-11, Revelation 3:1-3).French Jean François Millet gave hard labour its due, albeit a bit idealized. The Afro- American Jacob Lawrence was more matter of fact in showing the plight of the Black working woman in America: you scrub the Titanic wooden floor almost prostrate, rubbing with clorox chemical cleaning fluid that discolours even you yourself. Yet artist Lawrence has too much happy colour awareness to be a complainer. Lawrence would contest Qohelet's early bleak judgment of הבל: the kaleidoscopic press of city life—Bar, Funeral Home, Beauty Shoppe, church and Dance hall— have a fresh, jazzy upbeat spirit, closer to the later *Ecclesiastes* refrain, "Enjoy yourselves, fellows—remembering God takes note of your doings!" (*Ecclesiastes* 11:7-10). Why even funerals allow a sprightly gait and bright colours for those who have sung with Mahalia Jackson in church, "I'm gonna move on up a little higher.... "

Dancing girl, Paul Klee,
(1940), oil on cloth,
Chicago Art Institute.

Goya y Lucentes, *Los Capricios*
(1793-98) #53, Que pico de Oro!

Self-portrait with beret and turned-up collar,
Rembrandt, oil on canvas, 1659,
National Gallery of Art, Washington, D.C.

Swiss Paul Klee's *Dancing Girl* (1940) celebrates the naiveté and joy in corporeal movement especially young girls thrive on, as a wholesome moment in God's timing for our human lives. Age soon enough creeps up on a person, when the vicissitudes of disappointments Rembrandt experienced (*Ecclesiastes* 12:1) can blotch one's face and leave you with folded hands, quizzical, weather-beaten, seasoned, hurt but strong.

The Spanish Goya y Lucientes catalogues (left), in *Los Caprichos* (1796-98), the social and political evils of his day with a penetrating, capricious macabre humour: ignorance and sorcery, prostitution, inquisitorial lawless cruelty, academic humbug—patients rapt before a golden-tongued parrot who can discuss disease with ease but not cure their sicknesses.

Goya's *Los Desastres de la guerra* (1810-14) go deeper than caricature, and document, in *Y no hai remedio*, the utter desecration of human life by humans; the stench, in *Para eso habeis nacido*, and senseless waste of killing fields in war; the coarse, brutality toward women and children

Goya y Lucentes,
Los Desastres de la guerra (1810-14).
Y no hai remedio, No. 15.

Goya y Lucentes,
Los Desastres de la guerra (1810-14).
Para eso habeis nacido, No. 12.

Goya y Lucentes,
Los Desastres de la guerra (1810-14).
Enterra y callar, No. 18.

—the "oppressions" Qohelet saw (cf. *Ecclesiastes* 4:1-3; 5:8).

The raped woman *Vergewaltigt*, 1907, German artist Käthe Kollwitz found discarded by soldiers in the vegetation, and asked, "God, why don't You stop it!?" (cf. *Ecclesiastes* 2:17-23).

Georges Rouault, *Miserere et la guerre*, Plate VII (1926).

Georges Rouault, *Il seait si doux d'aimer*, Plate XIII (1926).

French Georges Rouault's series on *Miserere et la guerre* (1916-1926) depicts the gaunt, captive sorrow of so many abused men and women fleeing under the darkened sky of wartime. But

Vergewaltigt, Käthe Kollwitz (1907-1908).

Rouault captures also the final chapters of *Ecclesiastes*: *il serait si doux d'aimer*: "It would be so sweet to love" ... one another, like a stern mother who tenderly comforts her child, telling about the Creator God before the young have to go out where the older generation's hand points ... out into the world so full of human hatred (*Ecclesiastes* 7:29,12:1-7).

We old and young both can be grateful we will have heard the final Word of the Holy Spirit Wisdom voice of *Ecclesiastes* which enables a forgiven human creature of God to be authentic, that is, self-critically willing and able to give away passionately whatever treasure the saving Creator God has given you (11:1-6), deeply aware that good and evil are mixed up historically around us, and also within ourselves (cf. Romans 7-8). One can be authentic ... genuine, trustworthy, good ... because one remembers, that is, is very aware now that God is caring for each one us, as God's angel was sent to cuddle the frightened, worn-out Elijah once upon a time (I *Kings* 19:1-9). But a human person like the indefatigable Qohelet needs to be changed from the detective "I'll-figure-it-out, show-me!" sleuth into a more subdued, grateful hearer and follower of Wisdom, awed by God's presence in mountains, oceans, trees and animal creatures, ... at home in God's world under God's sun, ... awed by the same God's presence in this Holy-Spirited written Word, and compassionately embodied in the God-human, historical Jesus Christ (Romans 8:18-39).

God does really pick up the broken pieces of our lives, individually and communally in history, and does that often through the compassionate acts toward others by the community of those who follow Jesus'

lead, as well as others not expecting
rewards, but just for the joy of it
(Matthew 25:31-46, I Peter 2:21,
Hebrews 12:12-14)!

Susanna Oppliger,
Der Engel mit Elia (1998).

Britt Wiström, *Caritas*, 2006,
Chicago University Hospital,
Cancer Ward.

9

A PAIR OF EXHORTATIONS ON THE REFRAIN AND CLOSING CHAPTERS OF *ECCLESIASTES*

The Refrain of *Ecclesiastes 1:2-12, 2:18-3:15*

Preaching sermons, I believe, is meant to help a person understand the Bible in the festive communion of the saints, who hear the Bible speak God's directing Word for life.

This morning, more than half the sermon, you could say, comes before the Bible reading (of the book you were asked to read during the past week in preparation [so you really have read it already anyhow]), and there's just a little bit of sermon after the Bible reading. So please don't get nervous about the time; it won't be longer than usual.

I do this teaching introduction for a good reason. You could say about our Scripture for this Sunday and next what the apostle Peter says about parts of Paul's letters: "There are some things in Paul's letters," writes Peter (II Peter 3:16), "hard to understand, which uneducated and unsettled people twist to their own destruction, as they do with the rest of the Scriptures too."

I've got three points before the Scripture reading.

(1) You cannot understand God's Word of *Ecclesiastes* correctly as a Christian, I believe, if you don't have an idea of how to read the whole book of *Ecclesiastes* as a chapter of the whole Bible story that goes really and truly historically from Genesis 1 to Revelation 21.

The Bible tells us the great deeds of the LORD. The Bible tells us how God created everything good under the sun, from girls to birch trees, from worms and trout to angels, ice, and fire (Genesis 1:1-2:4, Psalm 104, Isaiah 40, Job 38-4).

The Bible tells us how God repented, how Jesus Christ wept, how the Holy Spirit grieves when people become comfortable in their sinful indulgence—before the great flood (Genesis 6:1-8), when God's people thought Christ's earthly kingdom meant control *über alles* and especially over the Romans (Luke 19:29-44, 24:21); when you and I keep on acting like secular fools (Ephesians 4:25-32, Hebrews 5:11-6:8), or when we do an Ananias and Sapphira cheat in the church (Acts 4:32-5:11).

The Bible tells us the great deeds of the LORD patiently saving people like family-man Noah, who liked his *borreltjes* (liquor) too much (Genesis 9:20-21), and Abram, who had money, no children, yet whom God used for a new, historical start (Genesis 15-18,21). The Bible tells us how the LORD used Rahab and Deborah, Mary and Lydia, to do God's Will on earth as it is done in heaven (Joshua 2, Judges 4-5, Luke 1:26-2:20, Acts 16:14-15).

When you know the whole Bible story you know the great deeds of the LORD, who used Egyptian-university-trained, lonely shepherd-tempered Moses to pastor the stiff-necked congregated nation of Jews for more than 40 years (Exodus 2-4,14; Numbers 20:12-13, Hebrews 11:24-27); who chose the gifted, young fellow David to write psalms and dances for God's people to sing and perform (II Samuel 6, for example, Psalms 2-32,34-38,40-41,72:18-20); who got a few fishermen with ordinary names like Pete, Jim and John to give Holy Spirited leadership on a daily basis in the church of Christ (Matthew 4:18-22, Acts 2:41-6:7); who converted the self-righteous zealot named Saul into the educated missionary Paul and led him to bring God's Word to those who were not kosher (Acts 9:1-31, Romans 11:11-16)....

Ecclesiastes of the Bible—you can count on it—tells us how God does things, what the LORD wants done, and how the awful, mighty Holy One of Jacob was later fully revealed in Jesus Christ, whose Spirit is afoot on earth since Pentecost happened about 2000 years ago in a large way: *Ecclesiastes* tells us how the Holy One deals with us often miserable creatures, expecting the Lord's coming again.

You've got to keep this God-focus when you read the Scriptures, or you'll get lost. The Bible is not a telephone book where you can look up verses to cure whatever ails you, to prove your pet peeves, or to twist to make yourself look good —that's the way sects always misuse God's holy Word. *Ecclesiastes* is about God's doing things, about the LORD's promising and delivering, providing and comforting us creatures in and out of temptation, sorrows, and joys.

(2) The second point is, God has given us the book of *Ecclesiastes*, written something like the book of *Job*, although *Ecclesiastes* seems more like a monologue than a dialogue. I have to explain that briefly. You know how it goes in the book of Job. One of Job's so-called friends makes an impassioned speech:

Job, you're suffering because you've sinned! It's God's punishment on your evil deeds—you deserve it! So confess that you are evil, maybe God'll stop it; and then be good, or you'll suffer some more (e.g. Job 4:6-11, 15:20-35, chapter 22).

At the end of the book of Job, however (42:7-8), God says that Job's "friends" were wrong in what they had said, godlessly stupid; their concerns to set Job straight had nothing to do with the "gospel."

Christ tried to make the same point to his disciples who had listened to the Pharisees too much when they asked, "Who sinned? this blind man himself or his parents?" If the guy goes bankrupt, he must have been greedy. If you have a car accident, how can it be 'no fault'? It must be somebody's fault.

Look, said Jesus, neither this blind man sinned nor his parents (in John 9). He has suffered blindness (John 9:3) so that the great deeds of God might be made clear in his life. Get busy doing the works of the LORD, who sent me—don't spend pious time figuring out who to blame —heal, help generously, give yourself to your neighbour while it's still day, before the night comes when nobody can do anything.

The Christ didn't want to lose time himself—it was the Sabbath— so he spit on the ground (got that?!), spit on the ground, made a patch of mud, put it on the poor man's eyes, and God gave him sight.

Then the Pharisees hollered, like Job's self-righteous friends, because Jesus did it on the Sabbath day.

Good night, said Jesus, if your jackass fell in a ditch, you wouldn't ask it, "Why'd you do that?" or wait a day to get it out. But you won't show as much compassion for your helpless neighbour, especially not on the do-nothing Sabbaths (cf. John 9, Luke 13:10-17, 14:1-6)? You heartless people, dressed in such clean, white, respectable clothes....

Most of the book of Job, most of its chapters, are corrected, partly by Job's speeches but especially by the LORD, briefly, at the end when God even corrects and accepts Job's humble plea and asks Job to pray for his friends, who wouldn't and couldn't really help him (Job 42:1-9). And you would really be mixed up, if you took the speech of Job's manly friends or the Pharisees' work-righteous talk that sounds so good sometimes (e.g. Job 5:17-27, 15:1-16, Luke 13:14) as if that were now what God's Word wants you to do.

This is relevant for understanding *Ecclesiastes* because *Ecclesiastes* is written in this back-and-forth idiom too, in the question-and-answer catechetical style the rabbi's used:

"Who do people say that I am?"

"Some say you are 'John the Baptist,' others say 'Elijah' or 'Jeremiah.'"

"Who do you believe I am?"

"You are the Christ, the Son of the living God," said Peter (Matthew 16:13-16). *Ecclesiastes* is written in the imaginative, question-and-answer, teaching by illustration and parable, the way King Solomon taught when he was still close to the LORD, filled with the Holy Spirit, a practising wise man, making God's Will known to the people in this vivifying, pedagogical way:

"Who of these two prostitutes is the mother of the living child?"

"Bring me a sword," said Solomon.

"Okay, cut the baby in two, and give a half to each lady."

Did Solomon mean it? Was he fooling? What kind of Bible is this anyhow (I Kings 3:16-28)?!

You don't understand God's Word in I Kings 3 unless you realize that that was the trained, wise-man teacher's way God's servant Solomon could make the point very imaginatively and concretely, what a mother's love means, and so discern the justice God wanted done in a messy situation, instead of rewarding deception. That's the way the LORD God had these poetic wisemen and wise women bring God's Rule to bear upon people's lives. That's holy wisdom in operation, doing God's Will in a kind of dramatic, what I call the "Yes, but" parable way of teaching..

So expect that *Ecclesiastes* will indeed be very hard to understand; that is, you will misunderstand it, I believe, if you suppose, for example, chapter 3 of *Ecclesiastes* means: there's a time for everything.

So when it's time to kill, kill 'em off, and when it's time to make peace, make peace and hold your memorial services, until it's time to kill again, and then go ahead—there's a time for everything...that's what the Bible says....

No, that's not the good news of God's Word. That's a cynical, Machiavellian idea, a bad reading and a godless faith, which directly contradicts what this church believes about providence, the providence of God (cf. *Heidelberg Catechism* Q/A #27). And that very cynical, sceptical, pessimist position is what lots of people think *Ecclesiastes* says. Then they apologize for it: "Well, it's only the *old* testament; they didn't know so much about Jesus Christ and the Holy Spirit...."

But that is not the Reformed way of reading the Word of God, booked by our covenanting LORD that is useful for disciplining us (cf. II Timothy 3:16-17) in doing what is right. **The whole Bible is God's**

Word today. So expect a back-and-forth business in *Ecclesiastes*, like an imaginative catechism in a way: the persistent, questioning Qohelet, who, like a disconsolate, frustrated Job figure, is trying to "figure out" what in God's world of human effort and trouble makes sense, because actually everything seems to end up הבל; and then you will hear the other holy God-answering voices and directing counsel spoken by the seven-fold refrain and what I discern as the Woman Wisdom voice countering Qohelet's honest, desperate search. That is, expect the Job-book kind of wise man/wise woman scenario, reflecting upon our historical turmoil while simultaneously listening and anticipating a corrective sounding of the LORD's comforting Word.

The final, brief point to prepare us to understand what we read in the book of *Ecclesiastes* is knowing when it was written and the graphic character of the Hebrew word הבל. Let me just say this now (and I'll hope to fill it out more later.)

(3) *Ecclesiastes* **was booked about the time when Alexander the Great went on his grand, world-conquering tour to crush the Persian empire.** That means *Ecclesiastes* was written down after the time of Daniel, after the exile and the return of the Jews to broken-down Jerusalem, when Haggai and Zechariah preached, "Build up the house and city of God again!" God put *Ecclesiastes* on the books after the days of Esther, who helped the Israelites defend themselves all over the Persian map when the descendant of Esau, Haman, tried to wipe out his brother Jacob's seed. *Ecclesiastes* was written under the Holy Spirit's leading after Ezra and Nehemiah had died. If you'd put the books of the Bible in chronological order, *Ecclesiastes* would come after the book of Malachi, in those empty pages between the Older and the Newer Testament.

Ecclesiastes was given to God's people when they were a dispersed nation. Even those around Jerusalem, mixed in near the collaborator-Samaritans they hated, were demoralized. Israel had no king, no true prophets; the high priests pulled rank and paraded around as if they were the party bosses, while the ordinary priests and scribes deteriorated largely into temple bureaucrats who did crossword puzzles with Leviticus.

"Is it lawful to pay taxes to the Persian satraps, or not? What would Moses say?" (cf. Mark 12:13-27).

"If you're only supposed to walk a stone's throw on the Sabbath, once you get that far, may you throw the stone again?"

That is, the leaders of God's people at this time of *Ecclesiastes*, around 350 BC, by and large, showed no vision; they were stymied; they tended the temple shop and kept up their customs, but the high priest and his buddies ruled the roost. God's perishing, believing folk, who couldn't put bread on the unemployed table, were disturbed, down-hearted, and beginning to wonder: is our history as the chosen people of Yahweh a farce? Is our Messianic mission on earth down the drain? Will the LORD God still redeem Israel, or have we had it?

The word הבל is used in the book of *Ecclesiastes* like spitting out a vulgar, half-cursing expression. הבל *(hebel)* originally means "a whiff of (bad) air," "flatulence." The Septuagint translated הבל as ματαιότης "a bombastic emptiness" (cf.Ephesians 4:17-19; II Peter 2:17-22, v.18), which the Vulgate turned into *vanitas vanitatum*, a critique of human pretension. "Vanity" has been taken to mean in modern times the affectation of importance men can falsely assume, or the primping of a woman before the mirror in her boudoir. But הבל is worse than human "vanity," and is used throughout the Older Testament to refer to idols, to no-gods, fake deities, worthless puffed-up impotencies, which the Bible has no compunction against likening to "passing gas." הבל, in a word, if you don't mind my saying it, means "a fart." That's the way the Bible pictures imposters of God—nauseous, gaseous, wasteful vapours like the enveloping choking exhaust which engulfs a pedestrian in the thick of massed idling cars in a traffic jam during rush hour on a clogged Toronto street—"vanity, הבל, going nowhere fast with a stifling Big Stink."

Think of Isaiah's inspired ridicule of idols (People cut down a tree, use half of it on which to cook their meal, and pray to the other half as if it be God! 44:1-20). Well, the prologue and epilogue of *Ecclesiastes* has the superlative 1:2, 12:8 (הבל הבלים), which means, in colloquial English, "The Most Enormous Puff Possible of Stinking Hot Air," condamnably so!

Now we are ready to read God's Word. Please follow in your Bibles, or just listen. The first verses, 2-11, of chapter 1 are a prologue to the whole book, in which the authoring editor sums up what Qohelet's initial beef is. Qohelet means "teacher-speaker-leader" of a qahal, "a community gathered to learn." Qohelet is like an imam, a rabbi, a wise man.

This is the Word of God:

1.2   Stinking hot air! Utter Nonsense! says Qohelet.
       It's all just a big fart!
1.3   What's a person got left after all his or her hard work?
       a person who does their damned best on this earth—what's left?!

1.4   The earth stays put forever,
       but a generation of men and women goes when another
       generation comes (onto the scene).
1.5   The sun too rises up shining only to fall down, hard pressed
       in fact to get back to the place where it must start over again.
1.6   And the wind blustering to the South, then fluttering back to
       the North, circling this way that away always crisscross
       doubling back and forth on itself—so tosses the wind.
1.7   All the rivers flow into the sea, yet the sea never gets full;
       so there the rivers go, flowing, flowing, flowing to the place
       where they always unfilling flow....
1.8   Everything, I tell you, every blasted thing
       —a person can't begin to relate them all;
       no eye finishes seeing, no ear finishes hearing it all—
       every thing is everlastingly, exhaustedly busy moving...
       (where to)?
1.9   What has been will be again, and
       what happened in the past will happen again:
       there is nothing new going on under the sun.
1.10   Or is there something you could say: "Look at this! something
       genuinely new!"
1.11   Nah. It was there already long ago, before our time.
       People today just ignore learning about earlier things.
       Things that are still to happen will not be remembered either
       by the people who come after those things.

And then the Qohelet-voice self enters the book with a first-person story:
    "Look, I'm a teacher. I have been a king over Israel in Jerusalem."

Let me just say this: the indefinite, low-key way that is said—"a king"—and the fact that no name is mentioned, lets the narrative suggest that this is like saying, "Once upon a time I was a king in Israel, and I said to myself, I'm going to become wise. So I tried beautiful, landscaped gardens, big bank accounts, a lot of study, wine-women-and-song [chapter 2], like old king Solomon (cf. I Kings 9-11); and you know what? It all added up to a big fat zero. You can't take it with you."

Continuing now at *Ecclesiastes:* 2:18-3:15:

2:18   I hated the whole business! Everything I had carefully,
        laboriously struggled for under the sun I hated,
        because (I knew) I had to
2:19   leave it to somebody else coming along later, and who knows
        whether that person will be sensible or a fellow who couldn't
        care less? But no matter which—that person gets it!
        That person shall dispose of the whole works,
        everything I slaved for, trying to be wise under the sun,
        there it goes—pfftt!
2:20   This is why, cringing deep inside, I dejectedly gave up
2:21   expecting anything from all my hard work on this earth.
        If a person toils intelligently, prudently, ably,
        only to drop it in the lap of a man who doesn't work for it
        at all—it's all yours!—what kind of farce is that?
        Right! it's a monstrous curse!
2:22   What's a man or woman get out of it? All this honest labour,
2:23   this conscientious striving to sweat it out here below,
        every day an endurance, the work a nagging tension
        so that even nights they can't quietly sleep—
        is that not a cursed stupidity? Total Nonsense?!

Now comes the refrain for the first time in the book, posed tentatively
half as a question, as I hear it:

2:24   **Is then the best thing (possible) with a man or a woman
        that they just eat and drink and become one
        who surprises oneself at finding joy in the job for the day?
        (—No! that can't be it…can it?)**

        Qohelet interrupts:
        Besides, I clearly saw that even such simple joys
        come only out of God's hand.

The refrain continues:
2.25   **For who can eat, who can relish (anything) apart from God?**
2:26   **It is God who gives wisdom, insight and joy to a man
        or a woman, one who pleases God.
        But to whoever remains thanklessly cold,
        God gives the trouble of collecting
        and stacking things up—so that God may give it away to**

someone who is lovely in the eye of God!

Qohelet asks:
So, (craving) simple joys is also misplaced activity,
a useless chase of hot air?

Now comes the voice of Wisdom:
3.1   There is a right time for everything, is there not?
        There seems to be time for every kind of activity
        under the sun:
3.2   time to give birth and time to die,
        time for planting, time for weeding out what was planted,
3.3   a time to kill and a time to heal,
        time to break down and time to build up,
3.4   time to weep and time to laugh,
        a time of mourning, and a time of dancing around,
3.5   time to throw stones and time to pick up stones,
        a time for embracing, and a time to keep yourself
        far away from embracing;
        (There seems to be)...
3.6   a time to struggle for something,
        and a time to give it up as lost;
        time to save things, and time to throw away things;
3.7   time to tear things to pieces, and time to sew things together;
        a time to keep quiet and a time to speak out;
3.8   time to love, time to hate;
        a time of close infighting, and a time of being at peace...
3.9   What's the use?
        What is left over of the labour to which a man or a woman
        exerts oneself?!
3.10   I have come to see through this miserable problem
        which God has given humans to bother them:
3.11   Everything God has ever done is very good,
        done at the right time; this timing—eternity—
        God has put at the heart of humans too
        (this does not mean humans can find out
        what God actually has been doing from beginning to end.)

Wisdom speaks here with the second time the refrain sounds
in the book:

3.12   I have come to understand
       that men and women can do nothing good themselves,
       that for a man or woman to be glad, to be well-off in their
       lives, for any person even to be able to eat and drink and
       enjoy themselves in the constant press
       and change of daily life: all this is purely a gift of God!
3.14   I have come to understand experientially that
       whatever God does lasts forever—
       nothing can be added to it and nothing
       can be taken away from it.
       God has set things up this way
       so that humans will stand in awe before God's presence.
3.15   Whatever is and will be has already been:
       God picks up the pieces!

That last verse 15, congregation, is special to me. I once had a Canadian
father whose sturdy son of 19, years ago, out jogging for exercise, dropped
dead of a heart attack. Shortly before, that son had written home about
a chapel I held on this verse 15 of chapter 3 at Trinity Christian College,
45 years ago. With tears in his eyes and holding that letter, a long time
after, the father said to me, "My boy was a good lad...God picks up...
the pieces."

Don't let anybody ever say this book is pessimistic! There is testimony, revelation, the grit of redeemed hope here in chapter 3:15, for example, for taking upon our lips, in the most desperate circumstances, that
is as sure and deep as Romans 8:28 or Job 19 when Job cries out, "Even
if the worms get my skin, even out of a body, I know I shall see God, I
know my Redeemer lives who will justify—has already justified—me,
come what may" (Job 19:25-27)!

A key to reading and understanding the thrust of the book of *Ecclesiastes* is to notice the refrain which punctuates the reflection at different
intervals. The sevenfold refrain is listed as the text in the order of worship
for this morning service, and we've read two of the texts so ... far: 2:24-
26, 3:12-13 with echo in 3:22, 5:18-20, 7:13-14, 8:15, 9:7-10, 11:7-10.
(Maybe you will want to reread the book before the exhortation next
week, aware of the fact. This refrain, along with the Wisdom voice, which
I hope to exposit, God willing, next Sunday, is the key that unlocks the
flavour of *Ecclesiastes*.)

The book of *Ecclesiastes* says a lot more than the refrain; but this refrain is the positive, corrective Good News, which outweighs, as it were,

gives contextual shaping to the questioning, frustrated laments of not being able to make sense out of the ups and downs of rags and riches, the rise of nincompoops and the fall of empires, the observational fact that good people and bad people all end up six feet deep; in fact, the good people often seem to get what the wicked deserve—oppression—while the evil people get what the good deserve—a happy life. It's all a farce, hot air, vanity, stinking meaninglessness!

Not true, says the book of *Ecclesiastes*, even as it lets the troubled voice of Qohelet vent its lived frustration.

If you ask the question of 1:3, repeated in 2:22 and 3:9 and through-out the book in all kinds of variations, "What's left over from all your labour to which a man or a woman exerts oneself day after day after day —what's it add up to?"

The developing answer is, "You can't figure it out yourself, man or woman, by looking and studying (8:16-17). It's not in human power to insure that what you do will last or even be satisfying! Only what God does (3:14) lasts forever. And God is the inscrutable, compassionate, gracious LORD of every creature under the sun. The Holy One, who abounds in goodness, forgiving what's wrong (cf. Exodus 34:6-7). And what the LORD in godly wisdom brings to bear upon your life is for the good of those who love God, says Scripture" (Romans 8:28).

The refrain of *Ecclesiastes* is very concrete (2:24, 3:13, 5:18, 8:15): Even suppose you've made yourself more than enough money, but your stomach can't keep anything down. Simply to enjoy bread and wine, its miraculous taste and healthy nourishment, is a great gift of God.

The comforting truth of the refrain within which people are invited to live, to suffer and die(!) is formulated in 7:(13-)14:

On good days be cheerful, and on bad days hang firmly onto this: God is the One who makes evil days too, as well as good days. This is why nobody can figure out, determine himself or herself, what will follow them.

Wait a minute —what kind of Bible is this (7:14)?! Cut the baby in half? Either you're white-washing evil (God does it), or you're justifying God for doing terrible things—in Pakistan, Darfur, downtown Mexico City....

No, says God's word of *Ecclesiastes* itself: you're trying to "figure it out"! Stop figuring, Qohelet, and start listening, awed by the Creator God, and learn to pray as if your life depended upon...the LORD, be-cause it does, and our Father in heaven hears righteous prayers (cf. James 5:13-18).

Ordinary life, says the *Ecclesiastes* refrain, the richly simple plea-sures afforded us living creatures, like sunshine and rain or snow, and a glass of cold water when it's hot and warm tea when it's cold, are gifts of God. When God gives you life-breath and a measure of health, simply be thankful, like a child, in the kingdom of God.

When you can have joy in your hard work, be aware existentially that both the joy and the trouble is still the LORD's hand holding your fragile life full of sweat and laughter, labour pains and tears (cf. Genesis 3:14-21), so faithfully and tenderly before God on the earth. Be thought-fully thankful. That mixture of gladness and hardy toil is God's historical gift so you may even forget how brief your life span is (*Ecclesiastes* 5:19-20), and you may spill it over to your neighbours (who may be without a job or clinically depressed), like the surplus of anointing oil spilled all over and down Aaron's beard and high-priestly robes (cf. Psalm 133).

And when you suffer pain, real trouble—medical, sexual, or what-ever—become afraid of failure, are scared of violent things real or imag-ined, when God seems to have forgotten you are covered by Psalm 91, and the terror at night and suicide bombers by day or the pestilence of cancer clutches at you, or one of the thousands collapsing next to you but not touching you—when it's your own child, husband or wife, or dearest friend—it is revealed to you, O man and woman, by the refrain of *Eccle-siastes*, that both health and sickness, prosperity and poverty, success and failure, life and death come to you not by chance but from the LORD's fatherly hand.

God doesn't do things the way we "figure" it. To save us sinful, dirty foreigners, the LORD in love sacrificed God's own Son (Romans 8:31-32), grafting us wild olive shoots into the tree with holy roots (Romans 11:17-24). To confound people who take pride in their achievements the LORD prefers to work God's wonders in women and men whom the world thinks are puny, ungainly misfits (I Corinthians 1:26-31). The LORD, says Hebrews 12:3-11 picking up Proverbs 3:11-12, disciplines the sons and daughters God loves; it's the bastards (That's also biblical language!—Hebrews 12:8) who go jauntily on their heedless way.

But, you say, "That's fine, LORD, discipline's okay, but what's got me hurts terribly—it's evil! The devil is real! Is this what I deserve?"

The Scriptures say, "God keeps your tears in a bottle" (Psalm 56:8), they are so precious to the LORD. "The blood of God's children is dear to God" (Psalm 72:14), and it costs our LORD God self anguish (cf. Luke 13:31-34). According to *Ecclesiastes,* God know the troubles you've seen, and the LORD tempts no one with evil (James 1:12-18) to curse

God and die (cf. Job 2:9); but our holy LORD may use the pulley of suffering to reveal, make real in your life, the decision to live by faith in Jesus Christ, who knows the LORD God alone is the only rock on which to rest.

When untimely death, torturous pain, calamitous wrong, handicapping illness, evil forces strike, you will be blessed in a lasting way if you can come to grit your teeth to say: the LORD gives and the LORD takes away—maybe you won't be able to add the last bit of Job's phrase, "Praised be the Name of the LORD," for years after, maybe never, this side of the grave. But that's all right: if you come to know in your hurt that the LORD your God is the one in charge, then what has been sowed and experienced in tears will be reaped and experienced in joy and laughter (Psalm 126), believe it or not, *Ecclesiastes*!

The Good News is that the ills of the world, that you were blinded or crippled, disappointed for years, done wrong by neighbours, waylaid by the devil, is not "because you deserved it" (the line of Job's friends), but "so that the great deeds of God might show up in your life" (*John* 9:3) as a living member of the body of Christ, among those who know and do show—by compassionate deed—that our mortal human life time is not הבל. The refrain in 9:7-10 says: Go eat your bread with gladness and drink your wine with a merry heart whenever God has been pleased so to bless your doings.

May your clothes sparkle bright at all times, and may your head never have to do without festive, perfuming oil.

Enjoy life with your beloved wife or husband as long as you live this fragile existence lent you under the sun, if that is allotted you in your life and labour that you trouble yourself so busily with in the world.

Whatever your hand finds to do (v10) (for enacting this gospel of the LORD's redeeming providence over the troubled earth), whatever your hand finds to do (in that task), do it with all your might, for there is nothing doing, no "figuring it all out," no knowledge, no wisdom, there in the grave where you are going....

Whatever God works in you and through you, as you are while you breathe (3:14)—shall last forever. And even at the grave side (3:15), backed up explicitly by the Newer Testament again and again, e.g., I Corinthians 15:12-58), remember and believe, "The LORD picks up the broken pieces."

Father in heaven,
Give us peace with what you provide us, each day at a time.

Make us holy enough so our prayers and cries get you
to stop the senseless evil that confronts us sometimes,
our colleagues, and our neighbours.
Don't let the devil make so much confusion, LORD.
Give us the vision to stop doing crossword puzzles on itty-bitty
things in the church, saving face and keeping grudges.
Teach us how to share your providence with those
who are scared all around us, or who lack bread
that keeps one alive, to know that security
and bread come from Your hand.
And as my wife once taught me to pray, LORD,
"please make us and our children strong
for when the hard times come"—we ask this for Jesus' sake.
Let everyone who will, say "Amen."

God's Gift It Is to Eat and Drink

Text based on *Ecclesiastes* 3:13-14, 7:14, 15, vers. Calvin Seerveld, 1985 ©   87 87 88
Tune: Bartholomaus Gesius, 1605   Machts mit mir

Closing chapters of the book of *Ecclesiastes*, 11:1-12:7

As you gathered from last week, especially when you read Bible books like *Job* or *Proverbs*, the *Song of Songs*, and *Ecclesiastes*, the connections and tone are so very important in the reading, because some verses are more important, so to speak, to get the point of the other verses. It is all God's Word, but as in a parable, these poetic books of Wisdom are God-breathed in a way we have to learn to read. But there is meat here to chew on that can wean our confessional lives from always needing to be breast-fed: we need to learn to eat solid food as well as milk, says Hebrews 5:11-14. We stay children of faith, on our knees when we read, listening to our heavenly Father speak; but we wish to mature in understanding what God says, so we grow in the discipleship of Jesus Christ.

Last week we heard *Ecclesiastes* say: the evil everywhere doesn't make sense! Does it? It seems as if there's more than "sufficient" evil for every day of your life (cf. Matthew 6:34)! However, when God gives you bread and the strength to enjoy it, accept it gladly from God's hand; and when evil caused by somebody's sin, the devil's interference, or God's punishment—they're all different, but they all hurt—when evil falls in your lap, take comfort, thank God, that the LORD is the one in charge. All things—said apostle (thorn-in-the-flesh) Paul—all things do work together for good for those who love God (Romans 8:28). *Ecclesiastes* gives anguished voice to what I Timothy 4:10 says: "...we keep on labouring and struggling because we have hope in the living God who is saviour (=provides) for all people, especially the believers." That's the way things are historically, says the Bible.

This morning we want to hear God speak from chapters 11:1-12:7. This section follows up the message of last week on the refrain of *Ecclesiastes*. But before we read Scripture, I should make an interpretive remark, although I cannot fully explain it until (for those who wish) we have a short question/answer time after coffee.

Along with the sevenfold refrain is a Woman Wisdom voice in the book of *Ecclesiastes*, whose message coincides with the refrain, as it were; but she gives key set speeches herself, like the chapter 3:1-15 "God picks up the pieces" revelation. A biblical precedent for the Woman Wisdom voice you can find in Proverbs 1:20-33 and chapter 8. Woman Wisdom's presence in the book of *Ecclesiastes* becomes dominant and conclusive in the book, in today's reading, the way God's voice in the book of *Job* resounds at the close of that book.

This is the liturgical season of creation, and "creation theology" is central to the Good News of *Ecclesiastes*; check out its refrain. But *Ecclesiastes* was booked, as I said last week, in bad times: Qohelet's firsthand observations note: (3:16) both the legal system and the temple organization are corrupt; (4:1) people below the poverty line get no help from anybody—those without work starve, and there's not much work in Jerusalem; (5:8) people are arbitrarily reassessed taxes and given tax cuts —it's payola all the way up the line, a crooked political network; (10:5-7) stupid people get appointments to high places, and princely fellows work in a hole in the basement; (10:20) espionage is complete; don't even trust the person you sleep with—a little bird might tell on you, your disapproval of the government;—it's like Holland during Nazi occupation with NSBers (informers) all around, or it's like the day coming when TV screens will monitor you everywhere, not only watching you in the subway stations, at bank teller machines, streets and in supermarkets, but also in meetings like church, even in your own home....

Our world today is fraught with similar evil. Troubles caused by our human sin persist, and often lead Christ's followers to stumble around in the dark. But the book of *Ecclesiastes* brings God's good news without wincing at our being smack in the midst of deep troubles. I'd like to ask us to sing Psalm 137 to get us together into the spirit of *Ecclesiastes'* setting again.

Psalm 137 recalls the terrible time when God's people were exiled; they had been deported as a subjugated people, were mocked for their faith; Jerusalem, the holy city ("heaven"), had been razed, burned to the ground....

The Welsh dirge melody we will sing has sackcloth and ashes in the tune. If we live into the desperate words, we can sing stanza 5, where God's weak, broken people plead for **the LORD** to do justice and finish off the systemic evil which has ruined them. Then we are close to the temper of *Ecclesiastes*.

How then shall we live? being renewed in God's Spirit to follow Jesus Christ? That is the instruction from *Ecclesiastes* 11:1-12:7.

Again, please follow closely in your NRSV translation, or just listen, since God's written Word is meant to be heard.

Psalm 137

Bab - y - lon streams re - ceived our tears:
Our cap - tors laughed, "Per - form your praise!
So help us, God, You may de - stroy
Re - mem - ber, LORD, the aw - ful day
God give you e - vil for re - ward.

Zi - on the ho - y cit - y gone.
Mer - ri - ly dance, Je - ru - sa - lem!"
our work - ing hands if we de - ny--
vi - o - lent E - dom cursed your folk:
Blest be the One who brings your fall

Ex - iles, we cried be - neath the trees.
How could we chant the LORD God's songs
strike our mouths mute if we ne - glect
"Bab - y - lon, break Je - ru - sa - lem!
Bab - y - lon Great-- your seed be damned!

Harps hung in si - lence man - y years.
while we were crushed in hea - thens' ways?
to make your cit - y our chief joy.
Raze to the ground, strip her a - way!"
Ven-geance shall come from God our LORD.

Text: Palm 137; vers. Calvin Seerveld, 1982   LM
Tune Griffith Hugh Jones, 1890   CLEF

This is the Woman Wisdom voice:

11.1   Go ahead, throw your bread freely out upon the face of
        the water, because after many,

11.2   many days you shall find it back again. That means: give
        away to many and more than many people whatever has
        been allotted you, for you don't really know at all what evil
        there is still to come upon the earth:

11.3   when the clouds get swollen with rain, they disgorge it upon
        the ground, and when a tree crashes to the earth southward,
        or if it happens to be northward, in the spot where the tree fell,
        there it lies.

11.4   Still: whoever always watches the wind (for fear it blow) never
        comes to sowing (the seed), and habitual cloud-watchers (for
        fear it rain) never gather in a harvest.

11.5   Just as you are never able to know experientially how the
        breath of life begins, like the little bones are formed deep within
        the womb of a woman filled with child, just so you shall never
        be able to come to know through and through the doings of
        God, the global mighty workings which God does.

11.6   Therefore, from crack of dawn to dusk, sow your seed and
        do not let your hand be idle, for you can never be knowing
        what precisely will work, whether this or that or both alike
        shall be worth doing

Here comes the seventh and final time the refrain of "Joy in God's creatural gifts" sounds in the book:

**11.7   Yes, "Sweet is the light, and pleasant to the eyes it is to
        experience the warming sun."**

**11.8   Yes, if a person lives many, many years, let him or her joy
        in them all:
        just let them not forget that the dark days, all those that
        come—an obscuring stinking mist (הבל)—shall be many too.**

**11.9   Enjoy yourself, fellow, while you are young! Let that red
        pulsing blood in you make you feel good that you are a
        young fellow. Do what you really feel like doing! Revel in
        whatever your eyes light upon—of course, know that in all
        these things, God will make you stand for judgment.**

11.10   Get rid of things that disturb you deep down! I hope you young fellows never get bodily sick, because being young, having a flourishing beard...is an idle preoccupation (הבל) soon past!

The concluding chapter begins with the reflective Woman Wisdom voice:

12.1   Remember the One who created you; think about that while you are a young fellow, before the evil days come, before the years creep up on you when you have to say, "That's not for me! I don't feel like it."

12.1   (Keep an eye open for your Creator) before the sunlight stops, and the moon and stars turn dark, and dirty black clouds cover (everything) again and again after pouring rain.

12.3   (Learn to recognize your Creator) before that Day when those who guard the house shall begin to tremble, and strong men will double themselves up (in fear); when women will stop working at the mill because too many have died, and those (left) looking out through the windows will fade away into the shadows;

12.4   when doors open to the street will be shut at the eerie noise of the mill grinding down; when the (distant) chittering of birds will give you gooseflesh, all the little girls who used to sing will have been stilled;

12.5   when people will even be scared to death of what's up in the air, and terrifying thing will take place on the street— although the almond tree will be blossoming—the grasshopper will hardly be able to drag itself over the ground, and the salty caper berry will be tasteless. (Get close to your Creator before that Day,) because then a man and a woman go to their eternal home, and those lamenting it will mill around in the street outside.

12.6   Get close to your Creator before the silver cord is taken away and the golden bowl is smashed to bits, before the pitcher near the spring of water is shattered and the waterwheel at the well is wrecked:

12.7   the dust turns back to dirt as it once was, and the breath of life turns back to God who once gave it ... (11:1-12:7).

This is the Word of the LORD!

I have three points again, and the third point is the Wisdom voice of paragraph 11:1-6, which I consider to be a climactic point of the book. But let me develop two other points first—the refrain again, and the meaning of the famous chapter 12.

First (1), depending on how you count it (if v.22 of chapter 3 is taken like an echo of 3:12-13), 11:7-10 is the seventh and last time the refrain is sounded in the book. It says in 11:7-10:

> Good days and wasted days will come your way. You who are young in body and heart, really enjoy those good times! That's right, even being proud of your body—the first time you can grow a beard or be seen as an attractive woman is great! There's a right time for such things, and they all too soon pass. So accept the pleasure of youth and naiveté when God gives them to you, knowing that there too God's firm, compassionate judgment is for the redeeming of your vibrant consciousness.

That's the way to hear the refrain, I believe, of 11:7-10.

If you study this book as well as read it, I think you will find that the refrain grows in certainty as one moves through the trials of chapter after chapter. The litany of frustrations and evils that are recited are countered by the testimony of God's wonderful providence of gifts, which grows ever more sure, determined, joyful, carefree and encompassing throughout the book.

The refrain in chapter 2:24-26 seems somewhat incredulous, wondering if it be indeed true that anybody who goes the route of chapters 1 and 2—wine, women, study, and song, or today we would say, booze, university, travel and shows, making killings on the stock market, building bigger and bigger barns (cf. Luke 12:13-21)—that all it adds up to (this secular North American way of life) is the death of more and more debts, pride, worries, wars, and frenetic emptiness inside the people caught in the ratrace for success, power, acclaim, and bankrupted happiness. The refrain asks in 2:24-26 in this literarily composed book with a refrain: does it mean the simple pleasures from God's hand outweigh the big-time stuff?

Could be.

The refrain in chapter 5:18-20 [English] later on follows the terrible chapter 4. You won't find anything in the Bible more despondent than 4:2-3: the dead are better off than those who are still breathing, says Qohelet; would to God I had never even breathed but been aborted!

That's pretty strong stuff in the Bible (cf. also 6:3-5), like Jeremiah's cursing the day he was born (Jeremiah 20:14-18); but it's so strong because of how desperately powerless this wiseman feels in God's world when he sees what 4:1 calls "oppressions"—"I saw the tears of the oppressed."

Do you just read past a word like that when you find it in the Bible —"oppressions"? I don't know what "oppressions" mean to you, but in *Ecclesiastes,* "oppressions" mean "cruel violations of defenceless people."

I saw somebody just raped, says the troubled believing voice of Qohelet in *Ecclesiastes,* cry uncontrollably. What could I do?

I saw a young fellow with a different ethnically coloured skin after he'd been beaten senseless in an alley by a group of thugs and left behind a shambles; they had worked his spine over with clubs, smashed and dislocated his bones for life. I didn't even know how to pick him up.

I've seen parents identify their child at the morgue, run over by a drunken driver, who was still laughing; and the big tears rolled wordless down their cheeks and fell in quiet drops on the ground—"oppressions"....

Then I saw people working hard, says Qohelet, the investigative teacher, and I thought, "At least that's something!" until I saw through it—they were being driven by covetousness, selfishness, wanting to be important (cf. 4:4-8).

And I saw people going to church (the begining of chapter 5) as a sacrifice to respectability, not eager to listen, to hear God's Word, the LORD's imperative, to listen breathlessly keyed up to hear what the Spirit is saying to the church! They were interested in nice things, like when the millennium will come, or speaking in tongues, or pleasant music, not in homes for battered wives or christian schooling for students who can get so mixed up in a secular setting they don't know the truth of what to live for from a hole in the ground. "Hallelu! Hallelu!" they sing, and haven't seen an "oppression" all week. They've never sat up all night with somebody who schizophrenically hears voices or has attempted suicide; they never saw the hopelessness from the inside of a jail; they've not once visited Christ at an orphanage or a nursing home where people suffer who have no family or friends, or done the endless committee work of the organized church.

But then the refrain of chapter 5:18-20 comes through more vigorously than in chapter 2 or 3, as if the worse things look, the more grateful the wiseman and wise woman will be in accepting the gift from God of quiet laughter inside one's difficult life. It is almost as if the more eye you have for oppression, the more sight you are given to thank God unconsciously for God's gifts, because you don't stay stuck in staring at the evils

(5:20) but offer the consolation of God's providence to your neighbour through your living trust in the LORD to come through in this life as well as in the life to come —it says in Luke 18:30 (ἐν τῷ καιρῷ τούτῳ)!

The refrain in 9:7-10, you know, adds marriage to the possible joyful gifts God makes available, not to sweeten the pill of daily work—God's not a pharmaceutical firm—but to double the strength and communion for those so blessed with the intimacy of a partner who are busy confront-ing evil in the task of reconciling the world new back to God in Jesus Christ, as Paul puts it (II Corinthians 5:17-19).

Well, the refrain in chapter 11:7-10 follows up the new dismay of chapters 8 and 9, where a softened-up Qohelet, who is recognizing better the limits of human knowing (8:16-9:1), experiences the failure of genuine wisdom to bring meaning, because nobody listens to it! (9:13-16). And Qohelet sees that the ruling government no longer rules, but is fundamen-tally only profiteering from its perks—raising their own salaries, attending conventions, spending time trading insults in the Commons, making al-most travel-brochure political promises in the mayoral election campaign (10:5-7): impending disaster for any truly God-fearing populace.

Be glad, says the refrain in chapter 11, in your youth! Enjoy being under 30 while you have it from God's hand. Don't let older people make fun of you because you think style is important, because you like to move your body around and have a beat to the music. Don't let older people despise your youth. Paul told Timothy, don't neglect the gifts God gave you, even if nobody seems to want them.

You find this in the great chapter 4 of I Timothy where the LORD says, "Everything created by God is good and is not to be rejected if it is received with thanksgiving and so consecrated by the Word of God and prayer (I Timothy 4:4-5).

Instead, Timothy, show the older people with guilty consciences, by your single-minded faith, purity, prayer and diligence, that you love God with your special gifts—maybe you'll even be able to help "save" some of the older generation (I Timothy 4:16) and give them a vision of what the new earth will be like!

Older people often think their ways are the norm. That's not so. Any more than the ways of the young are the norm. The call of the LORD to praise and to lament and to serve is the norm. If you people under 30 have had christian parents and have been truly nurtured by christian forming, educating—if your hearts are in the steady grip of the Holy Spirit—you may know how to do God's Will in our evil day in ways we parents never dreamed possible.

It is significant that the book of *Ecclesiastes* adds this "youth" dimension to the refrain at the climax—we'll see why in a minute—and then carries through on this "younger generation" business in the highly poetic chapter 12. I need to say something briefly about chapter 12, my (2) second point.

It says in (12:1): "Remember the One who created you in the days of your youthful vigour, before the evil days come, before the years creep up on you when you have to say, "It's not for me, I don't feel like it.""

"Remember your Creator" does not mean: think back and try to recall the doctrine of creation you learned as a child.

"Remember your Creator" means: "Spend time noticing **now** what your Creator God does; reflect on what your Creator God wants, promises, and gives now, and work it out before you have lost the strength of your manhood and the glory of being a vibrant woman, and before the evil days come."

Everybody realizes chapter 12 is talking about the end of something, and many people read it as a description of old age (The NIV study Bible does this) because early Jewish commentators started that tradition.

(12:3) "When the keepers of the house tremble" means, says the Talmud, "when your ribs get shaky"; "the grinders (a feminine plural word) cease" refers to losing your teeth. V.4, "the doors to the streets are shut" means "the pores of your skin don't function well, and it's hard to urinate." V.5, "the almond tree blossoms" refers to "the white hair of old age," and "the grasshopper dragging itself along" means, says the *Talmud*, "your hips hurt in walking," or another commentator thinks it means, "the movements of intercourse are difficult."

It'd be funny if it weren't so serious. Allegorical exegesis of Scripture is never trustworthy, because you can't check out what so-and-so thinks God intended because free-lance allegory has the text meaning something different than it says.

When you read chapter 12 straight the way we did it, not allegorically, then you can hear indeed the visionary, apocalyptic nuances of the text. V.2 is a clue the writer is talking about the end of the world: "When the sun and the moon and the stars are darkened" is the way Joel 3:9-21, Isaiah 13:6-22, Isaiah 24, Zephaniah 1:14-18, Matthew 24:29-31, and Revelation 6, all report the coming Day of the LORD, the final Day of Judgment, which is bad news for the wicked, good news for God's children, but also the terrible night when it's too late to work anymore in preparation for the Bridegroom's return (cf. Matthew 25:1-13).

Ecclesiastes 12 goes beyond the disturbed solar system of v.2 and projects in gripping poetic images (vv.3-6) the economic gnashing of teeth, the chill of fear striking inhabitants of cities behind their bolted doors, the curse of radioactive death-smelled hanging in the polluted air, and the breakdown of all artistic culture; *Ecclesiastes* 12 does it with a vividness matched only by the late chapters of Revelation (15-19) on the bowls of wrath and the fall of great Babylon.

It is so that whenever the failing of sun, moon, and stars to give light is depicted in the Older Testament of the Bible, it heralds an historical foreclosure on this or that world power or the Jewish nation; and we may expect something similar to hold here in *Ecclesiastes*. But all such prophetic, apocalyptic passages in the Bible don't just proclaim the impending doom God executes upon Assyria, Babylon, or old Israel, as a matter of fact for the corporate sin of the leadership in effect once upon a time. These apocalyptic passages carry overtones and dimensions of the LORD's over-arching, historical final judgment upon the leadership in nations today and in the body of newly covenanted Israel too, the worldwide Church (cf. Romans 4, Galatians 3:6-14, Hebrews 8-10).

The point of *Ecclesiastes* 12 for us, the Newer-Testamented body of Christ, is this: whoever has youthful vigour—before or after you reach 30 years of age—joy in your God-given, bodily strength to do what your Creator wants done before it's apocalypse now. Don't wait! Do your Creator's Will now while you have energy and time, before the cults and false religions muscle in to take over world affairs, and the saints in heaven step up their pleading with the LORD to split the skies unexpectedly (cf. Revelation 6:9-11, Matthew 24:36-41), drop heaven down on earth, and let Christ finally come to end the troubled work and loneliness and damage of the beleagured saints, and to wipe away all the tears (Revelation 21).

That brings us right on target to the final important third point, the urgent imperative of 11:1-6, to which everything I've laid before you from *Ecclesiastes* points. (I've got to try not to be too excited. The Scripture today is Holy Spirited dynamite!)

(3) The Word of *Ecclesiastes* 11 first came to the people of God in circumstances more oppressive than we can know in our Canadian land of milk and honey. (That's why Psalm 137 had to be sung and heard, to give us a sense of historical context.) As best I can determine it at this point, *Ecclesiastes* was booked during the time when Persian Ochus Artaxerxes III took over from his father by murdering most of his 100 brothers; he reconquered Egypt with despotic bravery (343 BC), subjected the ever rebellious Syrian satraps, and ruthlessly demolished the

theocracy, set up by the high priests in Judea c.350 BC.

That is, the powers of world-society at large c.350 BC were busy with political intrigue, in economic confusion, bloody and treacherous with opportunism as the Persian king and his generals fought against the disintegration of their worldly empire. The buffer zone of Canaan was continually bloodied. Trying to get out the the way of all the international turmoil, the Jewish leadership had the mentality of rolling God's people Israel up into a tight ball of "the holy nation," and presumed that the house of Aaron (not the house of David, and certainly not the priesthood of Melchizedek! in spite of Psalm 110), presumed that a privileged Aaronic elite in Jerusalem could speak as the authoritarian voice of God. The leaders of God's people decided to stand pat on doctrine, wait for better days in society, and prescribe every jot and title of an orthodox life.

Into such world-troubles and passive-a-faith community confessing the LORD came God's Word *Ecclesiastes*—can you imagine how that sounded? Chapter 11:1-6?

Since the Almighty provident LORD God rules historically over everything happening under the sun—this troubled, joyful, creaturely life we know—you people (11:1-2), **give away generously every gift your Creator has given you.**

Sure, things happen outside your control (v.3): wherever a tree falls, there it lies; whatever people always do, people always do. But don't just stand there (v.4) contemplating, "Hmmmm, so that's where the tree fell," or "Yes, yes, people always do that, so you've got to be careful."

Look, says vv.4-5, cloud-watchers, permanent on-lookers, "sceptics" really, foot-draggers, those so overly cautious in life they do practically nothing "new" because they misinterpret "counting the costs" (Luke 14:25-35) to mean "you have to be able to guarantee the consequences": such tedious cloud-watchers don't exhibit the leadership of faith, and they shall never reap a harvest. They are salt without bite and are pseudo-piously pretending to act for God, wanting to know exactly what will happen, or waiting to act until they do. But you can't know exactly which way the wind or the Spirit will blow next, or figure out how love forms the bones of a baby deep in the womb of a woman, i.e., how miraculously God may work God's mysterious great deeds.

So don't keep on testing, testing (v.4), testing which way the wind is blowing, people of God: sow your seed in the morning (v.6), sow it in the evening too, intensely; who knows which is better?! Sow your seed of faith, give away your talents, throw-away freely the richness of your gifts. Follow the LORD, and lead others in God's Way of deep-seated,

obedient, holy joy despite what hurts, and let God take care of the out-
come, the fall-out too, and the fruit of your passionate, giveaway labour.
You just be certain that you sow good unadulterated, Bible-organic seed,
faithfully unafraid, with insight, humbled, reforming, building, anticipating the LORD's return, up and off your christian fanny.

Sorry to say, it seems the liberating imperative of the Qohelet in
chapter 11 fell by and large historically into about as rocky a ground
as the seed of Jeremiah's prophecies did years before (cf. Jeremiah 11-
12,20,26,36-38,42-43). The Alexandrian Jews who did the Septuagint
translation of *Ecclesiastes* into Greek a hundred years after it was written
c.250 BC, thought that the refrain in *Ecclesiastes* described a hedonistic
temptation to be shunned along with the rest of the evils of the world.
Another hundred years later, the Essene sect near the Dead Sea believed
Ecclesiastes was canonic, but read it as a tract to bolster their ascetic pull-
back, the world-is-so-bad flight from being busy culturally caring for
God's world in history. Still a hundred years later, the apocryphal book
called "*Wisdom of Solomon*" (50 BC) openly criticizes *Ecclesiastes* for pro-
pounding nihilism (*Wisdom*, chapter 2), and teaches instead a Platonized
immortality-of-the-soul doctrine with a final judgment to pass out rewards and handicaps for your next spiritual life (*Wisdom*, chapters 3 and
6:17-19, 8:20-21, 9:15). So there is a long-standing interpretive tradition
of men (cf. Colossians 2:8) that hides, I believe, the gospel of *Ecclesiastes*
from God's people, *Ecclesiastes'* deep insight for our becoming closer to
God and more a channel of the risen Saviour, Jesus Christ.

I know, it's not my task to recite history, but to ask in closing: do
we hear the Word of the LORD for this Sunday and obey it? Christ criti-
cized the Jews of his day for searching the Scriptures lovelessly to find out
how to get/inherit(!) eternal life for themselves (cf. Luke 18:18!).

As a result, Moses, on whom you pin your hopes, will condemn you
(John 5:37-47), said Jesus, because you keep to the narrow way, binding
burdens on other people's backs (cf. Matthew 23:1-12) but have no eye
nor hand for helping those under "oppressions." (The priest and Levite
in the parable of the Good Samaritan were probably on their way to the
house of God to worship! cf. Luke 10:25-37).

That easily happens when people are on the sidelines (as students
and teachers often are) of where world action that alters civilization seems
to be happening, or are desperately hurting—physically, emotionally, in
their thought-world, confessionally (it makes little difference)—and are
intent upon saving their own necks: you tend to curl up in yourself, you're
less exposed, it seems safer, you want to simplify things, have spelled out

exactly what you should and should not do.

But then you forfeit the good gifts of God, given us under the sun, as you go about your necessary business, and you lose the healing joy that comes from responding to the LORD's imperative: giveaway whatever gifts I gave you, and you will receive your "bread" back…after a long while…multiplied, in this age too, even if it is with persecution (again, Luke 18:18-30 reinforces *Ecclesiastes* 11:1-6).

That's the sure promise of the provident, redeeming Creator, which *Ecclesiastes* leaves with us, and that's why the youthful generation is brought into the final refrain and apocalyptic picture: if we, while we have youthful strength, become and remain faithful channels of God's riches to us, whatever gift it be, then the LORD will see to it that those who are blessed by our giveaway ministry of reconciling others to the creaturely shalom God provides (and that includes new children of faith in our loins), then the LORD will see to it that the generation coming on strong will carry on and persevere with the bread of joy until Christ comes again.

The edge to the promise of chapters 11:1-2 is that if we don't give-away our gifts in Christ's Name, the LORD will take them away.

If we don't share the gift of the Spirit-filled Reformed faith we have, the meaty confession that knows the Older as well as the Newer Testament is God's rich Word; if we don't like to eat the solid food of *Heidelberg Catechism* teaching on "providence," the providence of God, and share it with our friends and others, then the LORD will take those matters away and make us a church that drinks a lot of milk, enthusiastically maybe, but that'll be it—pap, no solids.

If we as Christ's body and as church don't give Caesar—and that includes the current government in Ontario and Ottawa, the Persian Empire of stored nuclear bombs, the powerhouse of secular unions and university bureaucrats—what Caesar's got coming to him, not just taxes and a buttoned-up lip, but the Word of the LORD for justice, thrift, commonweal, educational truth and wisdom, moral and confessional freedom, help for the poor, then the LORD will take away from us even whatever gifts of justice, thrift, commonweal, wisdom, and freedom we had, buried in the ground (cf. Luke 19:11-27).

If we hoard our treasury of Genevan psalmody, pride ourselves on our commitment to an educated clergy with time to read and take sabbaticals, the heritage of trained musicians, the priesthood of every believer, but never exercise them in liturgical reform for fear of which way the wind is blowing, God will give us a deathly calm or scattered entertainment in worship services.

If we can't make a Sunday worship service for good reasons—"I've just gotten married and would like to spend some time with my wife," "I've just bought a second-hand cottage and have to get it in working order this weekend before the winter," "I've worked hard all week, and I'm tired out"—that's okay. But whoever has youthful energy and time and hears *Ecclesiastes* 11:1-6 ought to go out into the bushes and hedges of their neighbourhood parks and back alleys and bring in the people —the LORD likes a full house (cf. Luke 14:15-24) —to hear the good news!

The gospel of *Ecclesiastes* is very simple. It's just we slow-witted, foot-dragging creatures that are so devious. One could go on, but we'll stop.

We must not lapse into the confessional cramps and scholastic rote and uptight cloud-watching of the conservatist Pharisees of Christ's day anymore than we should catch the bug that spreads theological diarrhea liberal Sadducees have. Christ excoriated both Pharisees and Sadducees in Matthew 22-23, their play-it-safe policy of laissez-faire leadership, except when their own interests were at stake; and Christ follows up his anathema with the apocalyptic picture of Matthew 24-25, which really is announcing their being cut out of the tree of life with its holy roots, making room for grafted, wild olive shoots. Matthew 22-25 is an ominous replay of *Ecclesiastes* 11:1-12:7!

We must beware of our own leafy fig tree and its sparse fruit as well (cf. Luke 13:6-9). We only have one life to live before we face the grave or the LORD's spectacular return. What you do here Sunday after Sunday must never become just going through the motions. We come together, we are here right now, to hear the LORD our God speak to us from the Bible, speak discipline, comfort, and direction to us as a motley group of Chaucerian pilgrims waiting for the LORD to provide the manna we need through the coming week and that we are free(!) to giveaway to our neighbour.

Praise the LORD, our strength and shield!

Dear LORD, our Lord revealed in Jesus Christ
and the power of the Holy Spirit
touching us by the word of *Ecclesiastes*,
we thank You that whether we are up or down,
we can come back to You to get our loose ends tucked in again;
so we can go on as your children in the rough and ready world.

Please help especially the younger people here
to catch a sense of the fact that your Word is for real.
That when it comes to finding a job, a wife or husband,
knowing how to cope with sickness or success,
You, Lord, can lead us safely through the tempting
traps we like to set up for ourselves.
Whether we like school or not,
as we come to level with ourselves who we are,
it's crucial to have You, Lord, in on the deal.

For the older people here who know your providence
through *(de honger winter or)* hard times:
help the older ones, Lord, who need to relax
as they give themselves away,
so that Your faithfulness will be their constant blessing.
Bless the elders, deacons, the coming pastor,
and all their families. Bless the musicians
and custodians, the bulletin-maker,
servants who make coffee week after week.

Make us glad that what we do for one another
and for others is done as if You, Lord, are the one receiving
our gifts of love and time.

And we ask, dear LORD God, that You will teach us
thankfulness that we who follow Jesus Christ
are one body all over the world—
Africa, Asia, Australia, South America, the Near East,
Russia, Western Europe—and that your promises
in Scripture fulfilled in the resurrection
and second coming of our Lord Jesus
are sure, no matter what.

Amen.

Sculpture frieze (detail):
The listeners, Woodcarving in oak
Ernst Barlach, 1935
Ernst Barlach House, Hamburg

Barlach's Dancer, sculpted in wood, catches the mixture of absorbed joyful sorrow that graces much of his artwork. The unexpected, stilled composure of the figure radiates the internal restlessness of human nature, native also to the searching Qohelet figure of *Ecclesiastes.* There is a longing tentativity to our earthy existence that still expects, nevertheless, touches of peace.

10
PERSONAL POSTSCRIPT

Consider the Bible to be a phone call from God directly to you. And God is speaking passionately, slowly, and poetically to you, listening intently. Because God is polyglot, the accent to God's voice is somewhat strange. So God's long phone call, interrupted by your daily duties, is recorded, written down, transformed into text, literary text. It is a temptation then to just read the Bible rather than **hear** the LORD God speaking to you.

After I passed my doctoral exam for philosophy and Dutch literature at the Free University in Amsterdam (1955), and before I began work on my PhD dissertation on Benedetto Croce's aesthetics at the University of Rome, I followed the age-old European tradition of taking a *Wanderjahr*, a year off from your prescribed professional academic study, to see what else of interest was going on. So I went to Basel in Switzerland to study with theologian Karl Barth, philosopher Karl Jaspers, and New Testament scholar Oscar Cullmann, to learn biblical Hebrew, and to play university basketball and visit art musea with my social worker fiancée Inès Naudin ten Cate.

At that time my home church communion in the United States, the Christian Reformed Church, considered Karl Barth's theology to be "liberal 'neo'-orthodoxy." The normal evangelical judgment in America too was that Barth could not be trusted because he denied the Bible was God's Word; Barth said, "The Word of God is (only) **in** the Bible."

I found out that in Switzerland, Karl Barth was considered "conservative," thanks to his *Der Römerbrief* (1923). So I spent 3 months—besides thriving on exciting lectures and intriguing leisure—inching through a hundred pages of volume I,2 ¶19 of Barth's *Die Kirchiche Dogmatik* (1939) on *"Gottes Wort für die Kirche."* Here was my opportunity to beard the lion in his den, because you were allowed to make a half-hour appointment with Barth for a one-on-one question session. So I prepared well, had my series of questions in good German formulation written out—I was going to get him on whether he believed the Bible was indeed God's Word or not.

I posed my questions, made my critical arguments. Barth answered cogently and quashed my objections. In five minutes I was *erledigt* (emptied out, finished off). I still thought he was wrong, but I had nothing more to say. Barth was a genius and I was not. Barth was also very kind, and we talked out the half hour congenially until my time was up. But that half hour was a deeply educational experience, since it taught me that although you are worsted in a discussion, you may not be wrong—hold and review your ground.

Aftermath: during that year, for the first time in my adult life, Karl Barth made Jesus Christ real for me as the living Son of God on earth: it's not "Jesus" but always "Jesus Christ," Saviour of repentant sinners.

And it took me 10 years to understand finally what Barth meant about "the Word of God" and "the Bible." **The Bible itself is a dead letter until it is made existentially alive by the Holy Spirit's power when it is proclaimed aright with conviction.** The Bible is not God's infallible Word when it is self-righteously used as did the Pharisees and Sadducees of Jesus Christ's day (John 5:39-47), or misused by petty-minded argumentative Christians today. The biblical text has kerygmatic (proclamatory) bite and is a holy, convincing kiss when one hears God's voice calling out to any and everyone—me too—to become forgiven adopted children trusting and following the Lord's biblical direction.

This personal historical incident enters into and underlies my understanding of the intrinsic orality of the biblical text. The Bible is a pregnant script waiting to be given birth when its passages are contextually understood and given firm expectant voice. Vocal cords in the throat make sounds, but one's voice belongs to a person's whole bodied make-up. Your voice tells who you are; it is the societal passport of your identity; your whole being-there (*Dasein*) stands behind your speaking voice. So when God's convicting voice, filtered through Moses, David, Isaiah, King Lemuel's Mother, Matthew and Paul's reliable script, receives activation by your own committed voice, then God's voice has the reinforced opportunity to be heard afresh in the idiom of our own dated-located existence. Nothing is so compelling as to be addressed directly by the Almighty welcoming God of the universe in language you can in hearing spoken grasp to respond to.

Of course, much can go wrong when you pick up the Bible. You may not know how to read a fascinating literary script. You may not at first expect or believe that the biblical text is God-breathed, it is so humanly graphic in expression. The vernacular translation you have at hand may cut corners in order to give you a Readers Digest reduction of the original communication, oversimplified. Your life situation, emotional state, or swollen ears may introduce static into the phone call. If someone speaking Bible to you may be devious, it can be misleading. No matter, it is critical to do what sinner Saint Augustine said he did once when he fortuitously heard a neighbouring voice say, "*Tolle lege*"– Take up the book and yourself read (it aloud)!"

It will be helpful, in my judgment, for a novice Bible reader to have a little sense beforehand of what God is somewhat like. One needs to know God is affable. Almighty Creator God fully revealed in the historical humanly born God-man Jew Jesus Christ, who was willing to die to make good in God's sight for sinful humans, is at the core gracious, merciful, over-flowing in bonding love lasting for generations, slow to get angry at wickedness while remembering its occurrence (Exodus 34:6-7). So one may expect the biblical phone call to be inviting, unhurried, generous, bestowing genial insights, offering wisdom for the long haul, and waiting for a response.

That means the Ten Words of Exodus 20 reverberating in Deuteronomy 5 come through, not as stern prohibitions but as intimate hugs on how not to get hurt. Matthew 5-7 is not a revolutionary manifesto tearing traditions apart, but is a positive encouragement selflessly to go the extra mile for your neighbour. And the apocalyptic revelations of Ezekiel and Daniel and John on the island of Patmos are not scare-mongering predictions, but outlandish promises sparking hope and dedication. God's phone call is meant to give us meandering humans a taste for shalom.

And a final feature of the Bible I believe needs more recognition is the edited literary finish to its prose inscription of God's speaking to us mortals. I do not mean the Bible has the character of a novel. But even its straight-forward declarative sentences have an elliptical, imaginative coefficient. "In the beginning God created the sky expanse and the earth-world" is not stating in protocol fashion "a brute fact," but is telling us what actually happened in a way that any imaginative child would understand; so you do not have to ask "And how many years ago did it happen?" "In the beginning" means simply "Once upon a time"! And that Jesus Christ was born, lived as a Jewish rabbi, died under Pontius Pilate's crucifixion, was resurrected and ascended back to heaven where God's throne is, is not mythical or a fairy tale, but is true to life and is told with rhetorically nuanced, off-hand certainty to instill faith in the hearer of the testimony.

The Bible is not a potpourri of old disjoined fragments, but is a unified anthology of true history-tellings, prophetic discourse, songs (psalms) and letters, stories (parables) only the living God's Holy Spirit could have assembled, because the mysteries of our human nature and brief sojourns on earth are laid bare; our love and hate, aspirations and disappointments, sinful entrapment, and the rescue God has provided in Jesus Christ is truly told, you could say, with Dostoevskian subtlety (Samuel and Kings), John Dos Passos bluntness (Exodus, Gospel of Mark), Emily Dickinson's effortless simplicity (Ruth), and Ciceronian perorative eloquence (Romans), that is, with varied metaphorical éclat. God's quasi ventriloquistic mouthpieces of Egyptian-educated Moses, philosophical poet Isaiah, the apostle John, Gamaliel-trained Saul become Paul, and others, booked God's message with the stamp of literary quality.

On top of that, the Holy Spirit is no shucks as an editor either. For example, Psalm 88 is a desperate Korahite lyric put in between the upbeat Psalm 87 and persevering Ezrahite gem of Psalm 89, all of which are contexted by the orienting introductory key of Psalms 1 and 2, and a five-star joyful hallelujah conclusion of Psalms 146-150. Also, the Bible does not deal in caricatured heroes and villains, but hints at the wideness of God's incredible long-suffering mercy in reporting that King David, lynch pin in the ancestry of Jesus Christ (Matthew 1:1), adulterer, murderer, and desultory father, was nevertheless "a fellow after God's own heart" (I Samuel 13:14 and Acts 13:22). And Judas Iscariot, the Bible notes, "repented" (Matthew 27:3-5)!

The Bible is not a dogmatic treatise but is emblematic literature. Its very narrative character has the literary quality of being welcoming, provocative, allusive, **definitively suggestive**. The Bible is not fudging God's speech, but is telling us in open-ended brilliance how the LORD God in Jesus Christ is indeed dealing in merciful justice with us humans in God's historical world.

The book of *Ecclesiastes* witnesses to this God-speaking literary way of Biblical revelation I have been delineating. And you have to read *Ecclesiastes* as a chorus of jousting voices if you want to **hear** what God is saying. It's possible the young rabbis' spouting of proverbs corrected by Qohelet may not all be correctly assigned by me—can I always tell a well-worn truism from a fresh insightful conundrum?—but reading *Ecclesiastes* chapters 7 and 10 to be illustrating the limits of formulated rabbinic knowledge gives kerygmatic point to the juxtaposition of so many proverbs in this text. And just as you would misread the book of *Job* if you took Bildad's diatribes as the gospel truth and preached it to young believers to "Go and do likewise," so one needs to sense the tentative struggle in Qohelet's morose evaluation of what human effort amounts to—stinking hot air!—and interpret the refrain as more than a "carpe diem" sop to our human sorrows.

Letting us humans lament and grieve in faith, along with the Holy Spirit, at the terrible devastation sin sets loose in God's world, is a good news gift of *Ecclesiastes*. And when you come to understand that the final summation of the book—"Stand in awe of God and keep God's commandments!"—is not an authoritative put-down, but is a cheer!, then one is truly **hearing** in the script of *Ecclesiastes* the God who picks up the broken pieces of our lives and the history of the world.

Selected Bibliography

Aalders, G.Ch (1948) *Het Boek de Prediker*, Kampen: J.H. Kok

Alonso-Schökel, Luis (1963), *Estudios de Poética Hebrea*, in authorized translation as *Das Alte Testament als literarische Kunstwerk* (1971), Köln: J.P. Bochem.

Bartholomew, Craig G. (1998), *Reading Ecclesiastes. Old Testament Exegesis and Hermeneutical Theory.* Rome: Editrice Pontificio Istituto Biblico.

Bartholomew, Craig G. (2009), *Ecclesiastes.* Grand Rapids: Baker Academic.

Bartholomew, Craig G. (2020), "Qohelet as a Master of and Mastered by Metaphor." *Networks of Metaphor in the Hebrew Bible*, eds. Danilo Verde and Antie Labahn, Leeuven: Peeters), 329-346.

Barton, George Aaron (1908), *The Book of Ecclesiastes, International Critical Commentary.* Edinburgh: T. & T. Clark.

Brown, William P. (2000), *Ecclesiastes*, Louisville: John Knox Press.

Buber, Martin (1983), "The Heart Determines: Psalm 73" in *Theodicy in the Old Testament*, 109-118, ed., James L. Crenshaw, London: SPCK.

Castellino, George (1968), "Qoheleth and his Wisdom," *Catholic Biblical Quarterly*, 30: 15-28.

Childs, Brevard (1979), "*Ecclesiastes*" in *Introduction to the Old Testament as Scripture.* Philadelphia: Fortress Press, 580-589.

Crenshaw, James L. (1974), "The Eternal Gospel (Eccl. 3:11)," *Essays in Old Testament Ethics (J. Philip Hyatt, In Memoriam)*, eds. James L. Crenshaw and John T. Willis. New York: Ktav Publishing House, Inc., 25-55.

Crenshaw, James L. (1974), "Wisdom." *Old Testament Form Criticism*, ed. John H. Hayes. San Antonio, Trinity University Press, 225-264.

Crenshaw, James L. (1977), "In Search of Divine Presence," *Review and Expositor*, 74:353-369.

Crenshaw, James L. (1977), "The Human Dilemma and Literature of Dissent," *Tradition and Theology in the Old Testament*, ed. Douglas A. Knight. London: SPCK, 235-258.

Crenshaw, James L. (1987) "Murphy's Axiom: Every Gnomic Saying Needs a Balancing Corrective" in *The Listening Heart. Essays in Wisdom and the Psalms in honor of Roland E, Murphy*, 1-17, eds. K.G. Hoglund, E.F. Huwiler, J.T.Glass and R.W. Lee Sheffield: Academic Press.

Crenshaw, James L. (1987), *Ecclesiastes. A Commentary*, Philadelphia: The Westminster Press.

Delitzsch, Franz (1875), "Auslegung des Buchs Koheleth," *Biblischer Commentar über die Poetischen Bücher des Alten Testaments*, 4:225-436.

Dell, Katherine J. (1994), "*Ecclesiastes* as Wisdom: Consulting Early Interpreters," *Vetus Testamentum*, 44:3, 301-329.

Dell, Katharine and Will Kynes, eds. (2014), *Reading Ecclesiastes Intertextually.* London: Bloomsbury T&T Clark.

Dor-shav, Ethan (2008) "*Ecclesiastes*, Fleeting and Timeless, Part I, *Jewish Bible Quarterly*, 36:4, 211-221.

Dor-shav, Ethan (2009) *"Ecclesiastes,* Fleeting and Timeless, Part II, *Jewish Bible Quarterly,* 37:1,17-23.

Dubarle, A.M. (1946) "Qoheleth ou les Déceptions de l'"Expérience," in *Les Sages d'Israel,* 95-128. Paris: Les Éditions du Cerf.

Eaton, Michael A. (1983) *Ecclesiastes, an introduction and commentary,* Downers Grove: Inter-Varsity Press.

Eissfeldt, Otto (1934), *Einleitung in das Alte Testament:* translated by Peter R. Ackroyd, *The Old Testament, an Introduction* (1965). Oxford: Blackwell.

Ellul, Jacques (1987), *La raison d'être,* translated by Joyce Main Hanks as *Reason for Being. A Meditation on Ecclesiastes* (1990), Grand Rapids: William B. Eerdmans Publishing Company.

Farmer, Kathleen A (1991) *Who Knows What is Good? A Commentary on the Books of Proverbs and Ecclesiastes,* Grand Rapids: William B. Eerdmans Publishing Company.

Fisch, Harold (1988), *Poetry with a Purpose. Biblical Poetics and Interpretation.* Bloomington: Indiana University Press.

Fokkelman, Jan (1995) *Vertelkunst in de bijbel,* translated as *Reading Biblical Narrative* (1999) by Ineke Smit, Louisville: Westminster John Knox Press.

Fox, Michael V. (1977), "Frame-Narrative and Composition in the Book of Qoheleth," *Hebrew Union College Annual,* 48:83-106.

Fox, Michael V. (1989), *Qohelet and his Contradictions.* Sheffield: Academic Press, 1989.

Fox, Michael V. (2004), *The JPS Bible Commentary, Ecclesiastes* קהלת, Philadelphia: The Jewish Publication Society.

Friedländer, M. (1888) "Design and Contents of *Ecclesiastes," The Jewish Quarterly Review,* 1:1.29-47.

Garrett, Duane A. (1993) *The New American Commentary,* vol. 14, *Proverbs, Ecclesiastes, Song of Songs.* Nashville: Broadman Press, 253-279.

Gese, Hartmut (1963), "Die Krisis der Wesiheit bei Koheleth," *Les Sagesse du Proche-Orient Ancien.* Colloque de Strasbourg 1962, Paris: Presses Universitaire de France, 139-151.

Gese, Helmut (1977), "Tradition and Biblical Theology" (translated by Philip Ottara and D.A. Knight), *Tradition and Theology,* ed. Douglas A. Knight, 301-326.

Gordis, Robert (1944) "The Social Background of Wisdom Literature," *Hebrew Union College Annual,* 18:77-118.

Gordis, Robert (1951), *Koheleth—the Man and his World.* New York: The Jewish Theological Seminary of America.

Gordis, Robert (1976), *The Word and the Book. Studies in Biblical Language and Literature.* New York: Ktav Publishing House, Inc.

Greenwood, Kyle R. (2012) "Debating Wisdom: The Role of Voice in *Ecclesiastes," The Catholic Biblical Quarterly,* 74, 476-491.

Ingram, Doug (2013), "The Riddle of Qohelet and Qohelet the Riddler," *Journal for the Study of the Old Testament,* 37:485-509.

Johnston, Robert (1976), "'Confessions of a Workaholic': A Reappraisal of Qoheleth," *Catholic Biblical Quarterly*, 38:14-28.

Kidner, Derek (1976), *A Time to Mourn, and A Time to Dance, Ecclesiastes and
the Way of the World*. Downers Grove: Intervarsity Press.

Konrad Ehrlich (1996), "הבל—Metaphern der Nichtigkeit" in *Jedes Ding hat
seine Zeit. Studien zur israelielitischen und altorientalischen Weisheit. Diethelm Michel zum 65. Geburtsdag*, 49-64, eds. Anja A. Diesel, Reihhard G.
Lehmann, Eckhart Otto and Andreas Wagner. Berlin: Walter de Gruyter.

Lohfink, Norbert (1980), Qoheleth. *A Continental Commentary (2003)* translated by Sean McEvenue, Minneapolis: Fortress Press.

Loretz, Oswald (1964), *Qoheleth und der alter Orient, Untersuchungen zu Stil
und Theologischer Thematik des Buches Qohelet*. Freiburg: Herder.

McNeile, A.H. (1904), *An Introduction to Ecclesiastes*. Cambridge: University
Press.

Meek, Russell L. (2016) "Twentieth- and Twenty-first century Readings of Hebel in *Ecclesiastes*," *Currents in Biblical Research*, 14:279-297.

Michel, Diethelm (1988), *Qohelet*, Darmstadt: Wissenschaftliche Buch-ge-
sellschaft.

Michel, Diethelm (1989), *Untersuchungen zur Eigenart des Buches Qohelet*, Berlin: Walter de Gruyter.

Miller, Douglas B. (1998), "Qohelet's Symbolic Use of הבל," *Journal of Biblical
Literature*, 117:32, 437-454.

Moulton, Richard G. (1899), *The Literary Study of the Bible, An account of the
leading forms of literature represented in the Sacred Writings, intended for English readers*, Boston: D.Citteath & Company (revised edition of 1895).

Murphy, Roland E. (1979), "Qohelet's 'Quarrel' with the Fathers," *in From
Faith to Faith. Essays in honor of Donald G. Miller on his Seventieth Birthday*,
235-245, ed. Dikran Yltadidian, Pittsburgh: The Pickwick Press.

Murphy, Roland E. (1982), "Qoheleth interpreted: the Bearing of the Past on
the Present," *Vetus Testamentum*, 32:3, 331-337.

Murphy, Roland E. (1986), "History of Exegesis as a Hermeneutical Tool: The
Song of Songs," *Biblical Theology Bulletin*, 16:3, 87-91.

Murphy, Roland E. (1991), "On Translating *Ecclesiastes*," *The Catholic Biblical
Quarterly*, 53: 571-579.

Murphy, Roland E. (1992), *Ecclesiastes*, Dallas: Word Books.

Ogden, Graham S. (1977), "The 'Better'-proverbs (Tôb-Spruch) thetorical criticism, and Qoheleth," *Journal of Biblical Literature*, 96:4, 489-505.

Paulson, Gail Nord (1998), "The Use of Qoheleth in Bonhoeffer's Ethics," *Word
and World*, 18:3 (Summer), 307-313.

Payne, Michael (1988), "The Voices of *Ecclesiastes*," *College Literature*, 15:3, 262-
268.

Perry, T.A. (1993), *Dialogues with Kohelet. The Book of Ecclesiastes, translation
and commentary*. University Park: The Pennsylvania State University Press.

Podechard, E. (1912), *L'Ecclésiaste*. Paris: Librairie Victor Lecoffre.

Popma, K.J. (1961), *Heersende te Jerusalem*. Goes: Oosterbaan & Le Cointre N.V.

Reimer, Priscilla B. (1985), "A Time to keep silence—and a time to speak," Toronto: Institute for Christian Studies paper typescript, 28pp.

Salyer, Garry D. (2001), *Vain Rhetoric. Private Insight and Public Debate in Ecclesiastes*. Sheffield: Academic Press.

Sawyer, John F.A. (1975), "The Ruined House in *Ecclesiastes* 12: a reconstruction of the original parable," *Journal of Biblical Literature*, 94:4, 519-531.

Schoors, Antoon (2013), *Ecclesiastes*, Leuven: Peeters.

Scott, R.B.Y. (1965), *Proverbs and Ecclesiastes*. Garden City: Doubleday & Company.

Seerveld, Calvin (1963,1988), *The Greatest Song, in critique of Solomon*, 2nd edition. Toronto: Tuppence Press.

Seow, Choon-Leong (1997), *Ecclesiastes, a new translation with introduction and commentary*. The Anchor Bible. Toronto: Doubleday.

Sprangenberg, T.J.J. (1998), "A Century of Wrestling with Qophelet: The Research History of the Book Illustrated with a Discussion of Qoh 4,17-5,6" in *Qohelet in the Context of Wisdom*, 61-91, ed. A Schoors, Leuven: Uitgeverij Peeters.

Staples, W.E. (1943), "The `Vanity' of *Ecclesiastes*," *Journal of Near Eastern Studies*, 2:2, 95-104.

Steinmann, Jean (1955), *Ainsi Parlait Qohèlèt*, Paris: Les Édition du Cerf.

Treier, Daniel J. (2011), *Proverbs and Ecclesiastes*, Grand Rapids: Brazos Press, 119-237.

Whybray, R.N. (1978), "Qoheleth the Immoralist? (Qoh 7:16-17)," *Israelite Wisdom. Theological and Literary Essays in Honour of Samuel Terrien*, eds. John G. Gammie, Walter A Brueggemann, W. Lee Humphreys and James M. Ward. New York: Scholars Press, 191-204.

Whybray, R.N. (1982), "Qoheleth, Preacher of Joy," *Journal for the Study of the Old Testament*, 23, 87-98.

Witzenrath, Hagia (1979), *Süss ist das Licht ... Eine literaturwissenschaftliche Untersuchung zu Kohelet* 11.7-12.7. St. Ottilien: Eos Verlag.

Wright, Addison G. (1968), "The Riddle of the Sphinx: The Structure of the Book of Qoheleth," *Catholic Biblical Quarterly*, 30,313-334.

Wright, Addison G. (1980), "The Riddle of the Sphinx Revisited: Numerical Patterns in the Book of Qoheleth," *Catholic Biblical Quarterly*, 42:38-51.

Zimmerli, Walther (1962), *Prediger, Das Alte Testament Deutsch*. Göttingen: Vandenhoeck & Ruprecht. 16/1, 123-253.

Zimmerli, Walther (1974), "Das Buch Kohelet—Traktat oder Sentenzensammlung?" *Vetus Testamentum*, 24,221-230.

APPENDIX ON THE HERMENEUTICS OF HOLY SCRIPTURE WISDOM LITERATURE

My key to understanding the Bible is this:
    to realize that the Scriptures are **God-speaking literature**
    given to us **historically** for our learning by faith
    the one true story of the LORD's Rule acoming
    and the contours of (our) **obedient response.**
And the Holy Scriptures come at us whole bodily men and women compellingly in our total life activity today with that true story's directive:
    Praise the LORD! Repent and get adopted!
    Love your neighbour as yourself!
    Together reconcile all creation back to God in Jesus Christ!

Which call is to be heartfully accepted and concretely obeyed, on pain of life or death.

So there are four elements fused in my biblical hermeneutic method, if you will,
    (1) find the passage's **thread in the one true story narrative;**
    (2) discern its **literary configurations;**
    (3) get a sense of the **historical matrix;**
    (4) listen intently (on your knees) to its specific, convicting-enlightening **kerygmatic direction-message.**

People have different Bibles depending upon their stance/perspective apriori on (1) what is the true story of the Bible? No formula for Bible reading guarantees sound exegesis; the Bible's kerygmatic nature (4) defies a paint-by-number exposition. The text has to be prayerfully wrestled with in the communion of the saints under the leading of the Holy Spirit as to its historical matrix (3) and its literary contours (2) within the defining limits of (1) and (4).

    My own position on these matters within the historic Reformation tradition goes to (1) Acts 1:3; (2) Luke 16:16, 24:44; (3) Hebrews 1:1; and (4) II Timothy 3:16, Proverbs 1:2-6.*

Note: This hermeneutic method is exemplified in contrast to other ways of interpreting the Bible in Calvin Seerveld, *How to Read the Bible to Hear God Speak. A study in Numbers 22-24* (Toronto: Tuppence Press, 2003) xii-xiii. www.seerveld.com/tuppence.html

Proverbs 1-9
(1) God's will is revealed by the Wise who are skilled in telling para-ble-like metaphors and stories (Proverbs 1:2-6); cf. rabbi Jesus in the Newer Testament gospels (e.g., Matthew 13).

(2) *Meschalim* are gnomic poetry structured as "My student" paragraphs offset by hymns, other contrasting epigrammatic sayings, and speeches by Wisdom. There is a "Yes, But" interactive cast to this edited collection of disciplining educating (which normally marks the back-and-forth nature of how the Wise disclose God's will (cf. I Kings 3:16-28. book of Job, Matthew 5-7).

(3) Booked by wise King Solomon from early in his God-fearing rule (c.965-925 BC) [I Kings 4:29-34] about up to the time of the dedication of the temple (c. 953 BC) [I Kings 8].

(4) *Chokmah vs. kisil:* choose whom you will serve as a people (Deuteronomy 30:11-20)—LORD God's Way or your own "counsel" (Proverbs 1:7, 9:10). Cf. follow *Pneuma* or *Sarx* (Romans 8:1-11, Galatians 5:16-6:2).

The Greatest Song
(3) 6:4 discloses the date booked, c. 920-875 BC. God used the older wise counselors of King Solomon whose advice Rehoboam rejected (cf. I Kings 12:6-15) to book this critique of King Solomon's later days (cf. I Kings 9-11).

(2) Unity of the whole text with refrain
1:2-2:7 The Shulammite comes new to court harem and Solomon
2:8-3:5 Lover is searching for the Shulammite
3:6-4:7 Solomon makes advances to the Shulammite
4:8-5:1 Lover sings heart of love to the Shulammite
5:2-6:3 Shulammite dreams of Solomon's marriage threat
        vs. saving herself for her betrothed
6:4-8:4 Confrontation and resolution of love versus lust
8:5-14 Wise reflection on love with critique of Solomon

(1) Intertextual biblical connections: Proverbs 5:15-23, Hosea, Ephesians 5:21-33, for example, on the God-willed jealous, intimate bond of cove-nanted/betrothed erotic human love.

(4) Kerygmatic point focussed in *The Greatest Song*: 8:6-7.

Qohelet (*Ecclesiastes*)

2) Edited literary unity of the text with eye-witness reports counterbalanced by tentatively posited insights with a seven-fold refrain and voice of Woman Wisdom.

Subsectional development (roughly) within the biblical book Qohelet

The problem: What is left of a man or woman's work? 1:2-11
    search for answer as potentate   1:12-2:23
            (1) *refrain*   *2:24-26*
                  Wisdom speaks   **3:1-15**
            (2) *refrain*   *3:12-13,22*
Observations of evil   3:16
and [Digression: orthodox are
vain too]   4:17-5:6
Futile strivings   -6:9
            (3) *refrain*   5:18-20
How good and limited human
judgement can be   6:10-7:24
            (4) *refrain*   *7:14*
Truths "found out" with
further experiences   7:25-8:14
            (5) *refrain*   *8:15*
The problem recast
in God-dependence   8:19-9:12
            (6) *refrain*   *9:7-10*
Proverbs about foolishness corrected   9:13-10:20
           THE WAY to go in the problem   11:1-12:7
            (7) *refrain*   *11:7-10*
[Audience response]   12:8-14
           Delineation made by Calvin Seerveld, January 1973

3) Presence of "wise person" Qohelet (folk-assembly leader) in apparent absence of kings and prophets, plus mention of *beith ha'elohim** (5:1, Heb 4:17), and the described rootless turmoil (chapters 4-6) fit well with post-Nehemiah times, Alexander the Great era, c. 350 BC.

(1) That *Ecclesiastes* 5:4 practically quotes Deuteronomy 23:21-23 shows how Qohelet's "wisdom" respects תורה. Ubiquitous use of quoted proverbs, yet making the point of Job 28—true godly wisdom is unsearchable—situates the book of Qohelet firmly in the late rabbinical tradition Jesus restored to its pristine authority (Mark 1:22, Matthew 7:28-29. Cf. James 3:13-18).

(4) Woman Wisdom voice in 11:1-6, and 12:1-7, along with 12:13, was as fresh a proclamation to the uptight, defensive orthodoxic/orthopraxic post-exilic remnant of Israel (close in temper to the apocryphal writings?) as Jesus' teaching was to the Pharisees/Sadducees and crowds in Matthew 5-7, and is desperately needed to be heard today by our introverted and imperialistic Western Church.

I always miss Seerveld's literary voice in the gaps between his books. I miss the clarity and the biblical imagination that encourages and teaches us to listen with our own imaginations. He has listened to one of the most difficult voices in the Hebrew Bible, *Ecclesiastes*, and once again has opened up the book in a fresh way.

Michael Card, Bible teacher, song writer, Tennessee.

In this volume Cal Seeveld gives his reader a fascinating gift: an ingenious, literary reading of the book of *Ecclesiastes*, one that sets up an exegesis via its oral performance. The identification of voices—Qoholeth, the apprentice Rabbis, Woman Wisdom—and a contrapuntal seven-fold refrain that itself modulates in tone and texture, from a first tentative doxology to one filled with unabashed faith and hope, nuances our understanding of the thrust of this Wisdom book. We see here the same virtues on display that Seerveld earlier brought the *Song of Songs, Proverbs,* and the *Psalms.* The jewel at the centre is his robust retranslation of the Hebrew text. The jewel is set, so to speak, within the ring formed by an introduction orienting readers to the translation, a record of how it has been performed in worship, including the troubled questions it gave rise to, an example of how it preaches, how *Ecclesiastes* lensed eyes might see the cultural world and its visual monuments, and finally how letting it sink into one can transform one's spirit. These external contexts correspond to the internal intra-Scriptural contexts Seerveld so carefully brings to bear: the fit of *Ecclesiastes* in the redemptive-historical sweep of Scripture as a whole, the intertextuality that brings out a play of allusions, whether pointing retrospectively to the tradition of Scripture that the writer of *Ecclesiastes* inherits or prospectively toward what Seerveld calls the Newer Testament, both deepening the sense and nuance of individual sentences and paragraphs. This little book, like the translation and the oral declamation of the text it documents and cries out for, is a bravura performance.

Bob Sweetman, H. Evan Runner Chair in the History of Philosophy, Institute for Christian Studies, Toronto, Cross-appointed member of the faculty of the Department for the Study of Religion, University of Toronto, and Associate Fellow of the Pontifical Institute for Medieval Studies (Toronto).

The author of the book of Hebrews tells us that God's word is living and active—but it is Cal Seerveld who shows us how this word comes to life in Spirit-ed, head-turning, graphic, and visceral ways. His rendering of the book of *Ecclesiastes* not only arrests our attention as readers, it also invites a fresh response to this Two-Edged Sword that pierces joint and marrow down to the innermost places of our being. I dare anyone to read this translation of the "Philosopher" of the Bible and not be moved— moved to sober self-examination and to awe-filled worship.

W. David O. Taylor, Associate Professor of Theology and Culture, Fuller Theological Seminary, and author of *Open and Unafraid: The Psalms as a Guide to Life*.

Other books by Calvin Seerveld dealing with reading and hearing Scripture (see seerveld.com/tuppence.html)

─────────────────────────────

The Greatest Song, in critique of Solomon, freshly and literally translated from the Hebrew and arranged for oratorio performance (with original Gregorian style song composed by Ina Lohr) Toronto: Tuppence Press, (second edition) 1988, 107pp.

On Being Human. Imaging God in the Modern World (Burlington, Ontario: Welch Publishing Co.) 1988, 104pp.

Take Hold of God and Pull, fresh words from Scripture for our lives today [revised edition] edited by Elria Kwant (Carlisle, United Kingdom: Paternoster Press) 1999, xxi-237.

In the Fields of the Lord. A Seerveld Reader, edited by Craig Bartholomew (Carlisle, United Kingdom: Piquant) 2000, x-411.

How to Read the Bible to Hear God Speak. A study in Numbers 22-24 [a newly expanded edition] (Sioux Center: Dordt College Press) 2003, xiv-108.

Voicing God's Psalms (with CD readers) (Grand Rapids: William B. Eerdmans) 2005, 164pp.

The Gift of Genevan Psalmody for Today, sprung from its historical context (CD with lecture interspersed with songs, choir directed by Stephanie Martin (Toronto) 2011, 79:46 minutes.

Never Try to Arouse Erotic Love Until... The Song of Songs, in critique of Solomon: a study companion (Sioux Center: Dordt College Press) 2018, 106pp.

How to Read the Biblical Book of Proverbs: In Paragraphs (Sioux Center: Dordt Press) 2020, 189pp.

Biblical Studies & Wisdom for Living (Sioux Center: Dordt Press) 2020, xii-425.

Bewondering God's dumbfounding doings: God's talking to us little people in the final book of the Bible (Jordan Station, Ontario: Paideia Press) 2020, 163pp.

www.ingramcontent.com/pod-product-compliance
Lightning Source LLC
LaVergne TN
LVHW041257080426
835510LV00009B/766